Starting With the Destination in Mind

Creating Wealth in Any Economy

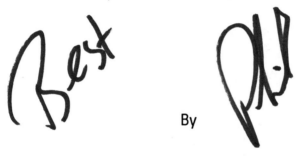

By

Philip Spillane, MBA, CFP®

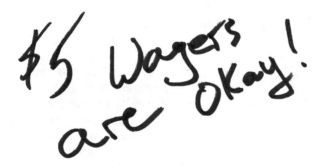

M⟲tivational PRESS®
LEADERS IN GLOBAL PUBLISHING

Published by Motivational Press, Inc.
2360 Corporate Circle
Suite 400
Henderson, NV 89074
www.MotivationalPress.com

Manufactured in the United States of America.

ISBN: 978-1-62865-031-0

Dedication

To Mary, Maura, Jack, and Diamond our Golden Retriever,
with love!

Acknowledgements

I would like to acknowledge my parents who provided unconditional love, but also set strict guidelines and limits. As an adult I have come to understand and appreciate that the word "no" really meant I love you!

My siblings Kevin, Kate, and "Mimi" who have made sure that none of us ever forget to consider others in our actions.

My Uncle David who taught me that my clients won't care how much I know until they know how much I really care!

Lisa aka Radar, my assistant and right hand, who has a knack for knowing what I need before I do; and her accomplice Bernie!

My clients for sharing their lives, celebrations and sometimes sadness. You are a constant reminder that we are never alone on this planet!

And, of course, Ann McIndoo, my Author's Coach, who got this book out of my head and into your hands.

Contents

Introduction

Since America was first discovered, individuals have been amassing great wealth from this land of abundance. A few titans of industry have created wealth in the billions of dollars, while countless thousands of others have created multi-million dollar individual and family wealth. So the question you might ask, "What is it that these individuals have that I don't?", or, "What is it that they've done that I haven't?"

Is it possible that these people have simply been lucky? I don't think so. Having looked at their stories, they didn't amass their fortunes over night; and speaking frankly, I don't think luck really exists, even though I'm guilty of using the term periodically. Success is a result of putting oneself in a position to achieve some clearly defined goal(s), whereas luck is something one wishes for, and requires no effort. For instance, winning a lottery jackpot where the odds are 1 in 170 million; that's luck. You simply buy a ticket then sit back and hope your number is pulled. By the way, if you think those are good odds, start counting in thousands and see how far you get before you tire, and then see how far away you are from counting to 170 million.

If it's not luck, is it superior intelligence? I'd have to again say no. Looking at successful individuals and studying their backgrounds, I've come to the conclusion that most of them are of average intelligence. Some of them never attended college, and more than a few never finished high school. Digging a little bit deeper, I discovered that some of these individuals also struggled with learning disabilities such as reading fluency, dyslexia, and Attention Deficit Disorder (ADD). Take a look at some of the most successful individuals with learning disorders: Henry Ford, the founder of Ford Motors; Richard Branson, founder of Virgin Brands e.g. Records, Airline etc; Charles Schwab of Schwab Investments; "Magic" Johnson, basketball superstar; and Walt Disney, of animated movie fame. Folks, the list of successful people with learning disabilities is exhaustive, do an internet search for Famous People with Learning Disabilities; you will be amazed!

Clearly it's not superior intelligence that drives wealth creation. In fact, my conclusion is that most successful people are plain old ordinary folks. However, as a Certified Financial Planner™ Professional and Investment Advisor, I do believe successful people share common characteristics and habits, which have helped me develop a process for others to build, protect, and ultimately distribute wealth that they never knew was possible. My process goes beyond the mechanics of investing, and goes deeper into the psychology of wealth creation.

If you commit to reading this book, and following the Wealth Building Task's, at the end of each chapter, my fervent belief is that you too can achieve wealth beyond what you currently imagine. However, I'm going to warn you upfront that this is not a get rich quick program, I don't think there is such a thing. Understand that there is no guarantee or promise that you'll be the next Rockefeller, but if you follow the program, which I present in plain easy to follow language, you'll be putting yourself in a position to achieve your goals and destinations, which until now were just a dream!

Chapter 1

Looking Through the Lens of Experience

"Change is Simply a Sign of Life"

My Story

Before we jump into the process, I want you to understand a little of my personal background. I don't want you to think I'm some guy talking from on high, trust me I wasn't born with a silver spoon in my mouth. In fact, I grew up in a small town in Vermont, the third of four children. In the early 1960's sociologists described our household as middle class. Today they dice up the classifications into sub-classes: upper middle-class, middle middle-class and lower middle-class. Back in the 1960's you were either rich, middle class or poor.

My parents were hard workers; they provided for us what they could and helped teach us the valuable difference between something one needs versus something one wants. With both parents working full time they were able to provide us with a comfortable home, a small three-bedroom ranch in a nice family neighborhood. We always had plenty of food, in fact my parents were sticklers about eating three square meals a day. Dad usually cooked breakfast consisting of eggs, toast and juice; lunch might be a sandwich and milk; and, at the end of the day my mother came home from work and cooked a meal that only Moms can make.

As far as our clothing was concerned, there was nothing extraordinary about our wardrobes. We never had designer clothing, and it wasn't unusual to get hand me down clothes from a sibling or relative. When we got older and felt the need to buy sneakers that were the latest fad, our parents would pay what they would have for the cheaper brand and allow us to make up the difference, using money we had saved.

The one thing in abundance in our middle-class home was love. My parents provided unconditional love for each and every one of their four children, which in retrospect was the greatest gift they could possibly give us. As with most families in the middle class, you always had a sense that money was tight, perhaps living in a small house lends itself to overhearing parents discuss money concerns. Knowing how much our parents loved us, we never asked them for things that they couldn't afford to buy us, for fear that it would break their hearts to say no.

From an early age, my siblings and I found jobs, I started working around the age of 10. There was a widow at the end of my street, Angie, who needed someone to mow her lawn during the summers, and shovel her driveway in the winters, jobs fit for a boy. Angie was a stickler for details, which meant that it usually took me two hours to mow and trim her very small yard. When I first started working for Angie, she didn't even have a gas powered mower, she had a push reel mower, and the blades were never sharp. Imagine a 10 year old trying to push a reel mower on an uneven yard with dull cutting blades; it was hard work.

At the end of two hours of mowing, Angie would come out of her home and reward me with a glass of water, or sometimes a glass of lemonade. As soon as I finished my drink she would hand me the hand grass shears so that I could trim along the edges of the yard and around trees and shrubs. Unfortunately for me, like the mower, the shears were never sharpened. When I finally finished the yard work, Angie would walk around her yard carefully inspecting my work, often pointing out "a blade or two" that I missed with the dull shears. After correcting my mistake, Angie would reach into her purse and pull out two shiny quarters. I was ecstatic, 50 cents for two hours of work!

A few years later I realized how woefully underpaid I was mowing grass and shoveling snow for Angie, but my parents insisted that I continue to work for her since she was a widow. But then again, this was the early 1960's and 50 cents could go a long way. After being paid, I'd walk to Tony's News Shop to see what I could afford to buy with those two shiny quarters. There were candy bars, soda pop, and even a bookstand that carried the latest Peanuts comic book. But usually after looking around the store and seeing what things cost, remembering that I just endured two hours of hard work, I walked out of the store empty handed and deposited my two quarters in a jar (piggy bank) at my house.

Eventually, the jar/piggy bank became filled, at which point my parents decided it was time for me to open up a bank savings account. They took me to the local bank where a teller explained how a passbook savings account worked and presented me with my very own savings passbook. I became fascinated with saving money. Each time I deposited money into my account, the bank teller would stamp two entries in my book. The first stamp indicated the amount of my deposit, and the second showed me how much interest the bank was paying me.

Imagine how pleased I was, the bank was being so kind as to hold and protect my money in their big vault and they were paying me interest. This process was absolutely fascinating to me, and a contributing factor to my choosing to become a CFP® and Investment Advisor.

Throughout those formative years I tried to make regular deposits into my bank account, but sometimes when I hadn't deposited money for a few months, I paid a visit to the bank teller to get my passbook updated, showing me interest I had earned since my previous visit. It was fantastic, like making money for doing nothing!

Later in life, as I studied finance and banking in college, I realized why the bank was willing to hold my money and pay me interest. You see, the bank was taking my deposits and lending the money to someone who might be buying a home, a car, or even starting a business, and then the bank charged the borrower interest for the loan. Note that the interest rate the bank charged the borrower was significantly higher than what the bank was paying me, and they were keeping the difference between the two rates as their profit, a profound concept!

I continued to do the lawn mowing and snow shoveling jobs as I got older, but once I reached the age of 15, I was legally allowed to work for minimum wage at a grocery store, bagging groceries and doing entry level work, whatever the manager told me to do. By the way, in those days you didn't have to ask the shopper if they wanted their groceries packed in a paper or plastic bag, there were only paper bags. With minimum wage and regular work hours, I was able to increase my savings nicely; something that I knew I had to do.

Growing up in my middle-class home I knew early in life that I was expected to go to college or a trade school after high school. My choice was pretty easy, since I didn't know the difference between a rip saw and a hacksaw; I was going to go to college. However, as a middle-class kid, that meant I would be responsible for paying for that education. And, even though I started saving money as early as ten years old, when it came time to send in a deposit to attend college, I realized I hadn't saved nearly enough.

I projected the total cost of four years of college and then deducted what I had saved over the years, as well as what I thought I might be able to earn working throughout college, and I realized I was going to come up short of funds. My options were either to take out large student loans, or to defer my admission to college for a year so I could save more money. At a time when my classmates were celebrating acceptance to college,

I made the decision to postpone my admission for a year. I didn't feel very good about having to delay college at the time, but looking back, it was one of the most financially prudent decisions I have ever made. Not only did I avoid the trap of excessive debt as a young adult, but a year of working full-time in a job I didn't like, gave me plenty of incentive to save aggressively so that I could go to college and prepare myself for a financially rewarding career.

I chose to study business administration at college. Why? Perhaps because I was a terrible science student, but also because I thought it would give me the best opportunity to earn a good living, allowing me to provide my family with some of the things that my parents couldn't.

When I finally graduated from college, I was met with an anemic U.S. economy, including double digit inflation and high unemployment. Yet, I was able to secure a job in the consumer goods industry, as a sales representative, selling personal care products. I went from poor college kid to someone making a very good salary, with annual bonus potential, and a company provided car; this was as close to nirvana as I'd ever been! But it got better; at the end of my first year of employment, I was informed by the benefits department that I was now eligible to enroll in the retirement savings program.

Since my parents didn't have a program like this, it was all new to me and I wasn't sure if I should enroll. This wasn't as simple as putting money in a bank, now I had to select mutual funds to invest in, and I was worried that I might lose money. I was fortunate to seek guidance and advice from a mentor within the company who told me not to lose sleep over picking mutual funds, since I had plenty of time to educate myself, but to enroll immediately to gain the benefits of tax-deferral, company contributions, and potential compound interest.

I did enroll in the retirement plan and was pleasantly surprised to find out that for every dollar I invested, the company would contribute a matching percentage, up to some limit which I have since forgotten. If you thought I was excited about seeing interest added to my bank account as a kid, this retirement savings program was like bank interest on steroids. The contributions from the company effectively gave me a doubling of my money even if my investments selections earned nothing. To my fortune this was the 1980's and the broad stock market was doing well, helping my portfolio grow by leaps and bounds. I was so intrigued by the growth of my investments that I began to read and study everything I could get my hands on relative to investing. I'd go to a book store and pick up magazines that defined the difference between growth and value stocks, junk bonds versus investment grade bonds. I started reading the Wall Street Journal front to back on a daily basis. And, on Friday nights I'd often stay home, while friends went out to bars, and I watched Lewis Rukeyser's Wall Street Week, television show. The more I studied and invested, the more consumed I became with building personal wealth, to the point that I finally decided to change my vocation.

Unfortunately, my choice to join a large national brokerage house was a complete mismatch. They were looking for an investment sales person while I expected to be an investment advisor. We were simply on two very different pages, such that after a few years of frustration, I left both the firm and the industry, retreating back to the consumer goods industry.

As the years moved along I continued to invest regularly into my own portfolio, adding a Masters Degree in Business Administration (MBA) along the way. Shortly before completing my MBA I was approached by a family member and offered an opportunity to join his investment advisory business in Vermont. Remembering my earlier experience with the large national brokerage firm, I made sure this opportunity was not a sales position but truly a financial planning and investment advisory position that would allow me to use the skills that I had developed over the years to help others reach their dreams.

I accepted the position in Vermont, which was the best career move I have ever made. I then completed the rigorous requirements to earn the designation of Certified Financial Planner™ Professional, approximately held by only 20% of all financial advisors.

From Advisor to Owner

One year after I joined the Vermont firm, now known as Bell Wealth Management, I was offered the opportunity to acquire a 50% interest in the business, and then a few years later I acquired the remaining 50% of the firm.

From the outset my goal was to serve clients needs first and foremost. And, as the owner of an independent advisory firm, I knew I wouldn't have to answer to an Ivory Tower (Corporate Management), which might not put the client first. During the first decade of ownership I renamed the firm Bell Wealth Management to clearly portray our mission and services. I also invested heavily into technology to support our clients varied needs and we moved to a hybrid advisory model incorporating fees in place of commissions, better aligning us on the same side of the table as our clients. During this second decade we plan to expand office locations so we can share our unique wealth management process with more people and help them in achieving their financial destinations.

Why This Book?

It is said that each of us has an area of genius, mine happens to be in financial planning and investment advising, which is my passion. I want to share my knowledge and experiences with others, beyond my client base. If my parents had somebody to coach them, or a book like this, maybe it would have made their journey through life a little easier.

I'm also concerned with the lack of financial literacy in our country, and wonder if it's a problem with the education system or just a lack of interest by individuals. My hope is that this book can serve as a break through. At a time when our middle-class appears to be sliding backwards, perhaps a book addressing wealth building strategies can fulfill the ancient proverb that says, "Give a man a fish and you feed him for a day. Teach a man to fish and you feed him for a lifetime."

There are many that argue our economy has changed forever and it's not possible for the average person to build wealth. They argue that manufacturing jobs with good pay and benefits have gone away forever. I would argue that we were an agrarian (farming) society before we became a manufacturing society, yet plenty of people made that transition and created tremendous wealth in the process. You can build wealth during the current economic transition to the digital age, you just need a process and belief in yourself.

Lastly, I'm writing this book because my parents taught each of their four children to be giving of ourselves, that's what a civilized society does. I wanted to share my knowledge and contribute a wealth building process, explained in an easy to understand form. Please consider this book my gift to you. My wish is that you bring the process described herein to life for yourself to create great wealth, and that you enjoy the fruits that accompany said wealth.

As you are reading this book, there may be times you might feel uncomfortable with the requirements, but what kind of gift would this be if I only told you what you wanted to hear versus what you need to hear? Building wealth isn't easy work, if it was, everyone would be wealthy.

You will need to commit yourself and commit to fundamental changes in your life. This is no different than if you needed to lose weight, you can't just wish weight away, you need to implement change to your daily routine.

If you're starting to get the feeling that maybe this book isn't for you, because you're afraid of change, read this powerful passage delivered by Steve Jobs, co-founder of Apple, to a graduating class at Stanford University:

"Remembering that I'll be dead soon is the most important tool I've ever encountered to help me make the big choices in life. Because almost everything, all external expectations, all pride, all fear of embarrassment or failure, these things just fall away in the face of death leaving only what is truly important. Remembering that you're going to die is the best way I know to avoid the trap of thinking you have something to lose. You're already naked, there's no reason not to follow your heart."

Steve delivered this passionate speech shortly after being diagnosed with pancreatic cancer. I keep a laminated copy of this speech in my pocket as a reminder to push myself beyond my own comfort zone, I hope it helps you too.

Wealth Building Task

You will find a Wealth Building Task at the end of each chapter, these are intended to provide a simple process for you to follow, one step at a time, with the goal of helping you toward your lives "Destinations". It is important to complete each of these simple tasks before moving to the next chapter, as they represent building blocks. Don't put pressure on yourself as you complete the tasks, no one will be grading you, except you! Also, understand many of these tasks can be completed in only a few minutes.

For those chapter tasks that ask you to write something down, you can use a notebook or separate piece of paper, or you can upload the free "Wealth Building Task" book found on my web site, www.philipspillane. com, under the Resource tab (Wealth Building Tasks), and save it to your computer hard drive. Saving the book on your computer will make it easier to edit or update your building blocks, as you proceed through each chapter of the book.

Wealth Building Task One: Write down a list of things you really want to change in your life relative to money; then write why you want to change them. Explain how these obstacles to wealth make you feel. For example, I want to get rid of my credit card debt which is currently at $2,000. I feel terrible each month when the bill comes in; it keeps me awake at night knowing I'm paying x% interest. With this debt I can't qualify for a mortgage.

Chapter 2

In God We Trust

"Every morning in Africa a gazelle wakes up,
it knows it must run faster than the fastest lion or it will be killed.
Every morning in Africa a lion wakes up,
it knows it must run faster than the slowest gazelle or it will starve to
death.
It does not matter whether you are a lion or a gazelle
but when the sun comes up, you'd better be running."

Have Faith in Yourself

As you begin the process of building wealth, it's only normal to feel a little intimidated, perhaps because you don't have a background in finance and you don't understand the many financial terms that are used. Undoubtedly, it was not appealing in the past when you turned on the TV to a financial program where people were talking in a foreign language using terms like carry trade and arbitrage. They use terms not in most peoples' lexicon (language inventory). And, instead of explaining these terms to the viewer, they keep firing additional terms that you don't understand, and before long you're changing the channel to a rerun of The Andy Griffith Show. My guess is that the TV hosts assume that if you are watching, then you must understand their language. The problem is that people like me who do understand their language are working, not watching TV. They would serve themselves and their audiences better if they took time to explain things to their audience.

Know that just because you don't understand finance or its terminology, you are not stupid, perhaps just ignorant. Don't take offense, ignorance is simply a lack of knowledge. If I walked into a medical office and heard a doctor discussing a right hemorrhagic epitasis, I wouldn't know that they're talking about a nose bleed of the right nostril. The only reason I know this is because my wife is a medical professional. There are people in every profession that want to sound more important, or smarter, than you and I. Perhaps they do it because they are insecure, and don't want us to know it, or perhaps they just don't realize what they're doing. Since we all put our pants on one leg at a time, or in the words of a former college professor, "God don't make no junk," you should understand that you are likely every bit as smart as those on TV, your education just took you in a different direction. So, my promise to you is that I have written this book using language that is understandable, so relax; there is no reason to feel intimidated. Why would I give you a gift that you can't use and enjoy? The only stupid thing you could do after buying this book is not reading it completely! Or as Forrest Gump's mother would say, "Stupid is as stupid does."

Keep in mind that the goal of this book is not to turn you into a hedge fund manager (a hedge fund can invest or trade in a wide range of things and generally isn't available to all investors), it's to help you understand where and what you want to achieve in your lifetime (that requires time, money, and planning), and to give you a process to attain your goals. If you're too nervous or intimidated to continue reading this book, go back and reread the passage from Steve Jobs and remember, we're all going to be dead a long time, so why not move forward?

Getting Out of Your Comfort Zone

If you really want something that you've never had before, you're going to have to do something different, i.e. change. Personal opinion here, but I think you ought to reread that last sentence, and give it some thought. I know change can be frightening, but if it leads to a goal isn't it worth it? I want to challenge you, from this point forward, to push yourself outside of your comfort zone, and don't worry about stumbling. Metaphorically speaking, it's not a big deal if you scrape your knee, that's what they make band aids for.

Since we are the sum of our life experiences, if you haven't had success building wealth in the past, you probably have programmed your mind to think it's not possible. Think back to when you learned to ride a bicycle. I remember thinking that riding a bike looked really easy. However, when I got on my first bike, and either mom or dad held me up until I could start pedaling, I found out otherwise.

My experience went something like this: Crash, Boom, Bang! Or as my grandmother would say, "I went ass over tea kettle." I could have given up after that first crash, but I wanted to learn to ride a bike, like my siblings and friends. I had to push myself out of my comfort zone, skinned knees and all, and try again. And, the next time I rode the bike I went a little further before I crashed. Because I didn't give up, I eventually "got it". Imagine if I had given up after crashing several times? I would have missed so many positive experiences, like riding in the Pan Mass Challenge (a two day bike ride across Massachusetts, raising funds for the Dana-Farber Cancer Institute), or as my friends might kid me, finishing behind a guy riding a mountain bike in a biathlon.

One technique to help you get out of your comfort zone is to redefine failures as successes. For instance, in baseball if a player gets a hit three times out of ten "at bats" some would say that the player had a failure rate of .700% (3/10). However, because the process of getting a hit in baseball is so difficult, baseball players and followers would say the player had a success rate of .300%. Guess what? A player batting .300% is considered an all-star!

Let's try another example of redefining failure as success. Tell me how I do on this little bit of arithmetic: One plus one equals two, two plus two equals four, three plus three equals five, four plus four equals eight, five plus five equals ten. Okay, how'd I do? Yea, I know, you're sitting there thinking, "Wait a minute Spillane, you're going to teach me about finance and building wealth, and you didn't know that three plus three doesn't equal five?" Well of course I did, but what I wanted to illustrate is that you immediately seized on my ONE incorrect answer. But if we want to redefine my failure as a success, lets recognize that I correctly answered four out of five, which means I earned a grade of 80% (4/5). When I went to school, 80% was considered a B-; and for a kid who didn't like school as a youngster, I would have been ecstatic to receive a grade of B-. Learn not to beat yourself up if you make a mistake and frame your experiences as successes, not failures.

As important as it is to redefine failures as successes, you need to learn to celebrate your wins (successes), and learn from losses (unanticipated outcomes). Know that even the most successful and wealthiest people have experienced failures. The difference is that if you ask them about their failures, they are likely to tell you what they learned from the event and how they used the experience to achieve other goals, rather than dwelling on the failure itself. The advice given by Tony Horton, on my workout videos, says it correctly, "Just do your best and forget the rest". Embrace change; redefine failures as successes, and become an all-star wealth builder!

Don't Count on Uncle Sam

To put it mildly, the twenty-first century has been a financial challenge for many. Already we have endured multiple recessions and the economy has experienced the loss of thousands of jobs. Families have sacrificed to send their children to college, only to have them graduate unemployed or underemployed, and often moving back in with their parents. Fathers and mothers that are financial providers have experienced the humiliation of being downsized or right-sized; tough times for sure. But I want to remind you that Uncle Sam is not your long-term solution. Government entitlement programs are designed to make sure individuals and families don't go hungry, and have a roof over their heads. The danger of these programs is that the longer people are on them, the harder it is to get back on your own feet. I realize that there are far too many situations where an individual is better off financially by staying on an entitlement program than taking a lesser paying job, but you need to understand that there are no promotions when you're on government assistance. I am not telling anyone that if circumstances require you take assistance that you shouldn't, I am suggesting that it might be in your long-term best interest to take a lesser paying job rather than stay on government assistance. You might have to take on multiple jobs to make ends meet, but think about how an employer, current or future, will evaluate you versus the individual that chooses to stay on government assistance. Simply stated, working puts you in the position to be recognized for additional responsibilities and increased earnings.

Take personal responsibility for you and your family; understand that no one owes you anything. They don't owe you a job, they don't owe you a salary, they don't owe you the best shift or the best hours, these are all things that are earned.

Know that if you have a clear picture of what you want, and when you want it, if you're willing to work hard, opportunities still do exist in this country.

The first thing everyone must do is complete their high school education. If you've dropped out, go back. If you can't go back to school, get a General Education Development Certificate (GED). Next, decide what you want to do for a career. If your choice requires a college education, go to college. If you don't know exactly what you want to study in college, but you know you will eventually need that degree, attend a community college. Take courses in different subjects to help you decide where your career interest lay. The cost of attending community college is generally far less than at a four year college or university, and the credits you earn at these two year schools should be transferable to a four year college/university. Note, that if you do transfer from a community college, when you graduate from the four year school; the diploma has the name of the school you finished at, not the school where you started. If college isn't for you, you need to find a trade school, or an apprenticeship program. I realize apprenticeship programs are not as plentiful as they once were, so, how about approaching a potential employer and asking them if you could work for free for two weeks. That'll get their attention. Tell them that at the end of two weeks, if they like your job performance, that they will agree to offer you full time employment. But, if you don't meet their expectations, you'll agree to shake their hand and move on. Baring liability issues for the employer, who wouldn't want to try this approach to see if there is a fit for both employer and employee?

Lastly, don't forget the military option! (a.) You might take courses while in the military that can lead to a career after completing your commitment. (b.) The military might promise to pay some or all of your educational costs, post military commitment. As they say, "Be all you can be!"

Respect Money

In the 1960's the Beatles, a musical group for those of you too young to know them, sang, "Money can't buy you love," and they were absolutely correct. But money is a means to an end. Most of the things in life that we seek have a monetary cost. So let's discuss money and why you need to have respect for it in order to attract and accumulate enough of it to pay for the things you decide are your life's destinations (goals).

A number of years ago I walked into a convenience store and observed a customer putting change from a purchase into a cup in front of the cash register. I was a little baffled because I didn't see a sign on the cup requesting donations for any cause, but I quickly put it out of my mind. A few weeks later I watched another consumer do the same thing at a different convenience store. Still not understanding why these people were putting their change into an unmarked cup, I asked the cashier about it.

He proceeded to explain that the change in the tray was for people that are either a little short of money for their purchase, or for those who don't want to carry change in their pockets. You might call me cheap, but I think this is the most ludicrous thing I've ever seen; effectively, people are giving away their money. I guess they think only paper money has any worth. If you've worked hard for your money, why wouldn't you keep your change and put it into a cup, jar, or bucket of your own? When your container gets full you could bring the change to a bank and convert it to paper money. Coins might be less convenient than paper money, but it's still money. Just think, if you put "your" change into "your" cup at the end of each day, you might find that you can save as much as $200 a year. Imagine one day finding two hundred dollars in bills on the ground? You could use it to pay off a nagging bill, or use it during a vacation to do something extra special for yourself, a spouse, or children. Pay yourself!

Here's a true story about a man in Massachusetts and his respect for money. Years ago he purchased a home by borrowing money, carrying a mortgage, and he said to his wife that someday he was going to pay off his mortgage in pennies. Over the years he started saving pennies and putting them into a container. He put pennies that he received as change from transactions into his container, and when he saw a penny on the ground he picked it up and deposited it into his container. Finally, after many years of mortgage payments, he proudly walked into the bank and turned in something in the neighborhood of 62,000 pennies, which represented his final mortgage payment. This is an example of someone that had a very clear picture of his destination to be debt free and own his home outright. Rather than leave his change in a cup in front of some cash register, he respected the value of even the lowly penny, such that it paid off his mortgage.

How often do you see a penny on the ground and walk by it? You can't buy much for a penny, but if you have a clear picture of what you want, and you are patient, the pennies will add up. Picking up just one penny per day can amount to $3.65 a year. Not much, but if you did the same thing with a nickel, dime, and quarter each day, you would have an incremental $149.65 to spend at the end of the year. More importantly, the act of reaching down and picking up loose change creates both a savings habit and a real respect for money that are the seeds of wealth creation.

Pennies aren't just found on the ground, they can be found by balancing your checking and savings accounts, or by carefully reviewing bills such as your credit card statement. I know you want to tell me that mistakes on these statements don't happen because they're generated from a computer. That's not true. I learned from a computer programming class in college the valuable phrase, garbage in – garbage out. Programmers, or those that do data input work, sometimes make mistakes, and if you are not taking a few minutes to review your statements; you are losing pennies, nickels, dimes, quarters, and probably dollars. In addition to input errors there are plenty of examples of fraudulent charges on credit card statements that are for small dollar purchases. These purchases are just small enough that those that don't check their bills closely will never detect, and they can go on monthly for years, adding up to thousands of dollars.

I have terrible handwriting; such that no Catholic Nun could improve. When I write a check, yes I'm old fashioned and still write checks, the number three is sometimes interpreted as an eight. Imagine writing a check for $10.33 and having the bank processor charge me $10.88. Now imagine writing a check for $300 that is input as $800. Checking my statements has saved me thousands of dollars over the years.

Would you like some other ways to pick-up pennies? Take a look at your cell phone bill each month, particularly if you have a data plan. If you're not checking your data plan usage, you won't notice when you have exceeded your plan limits, which results in a financial penalty. By checking your bill regularly you might discover that you have a plan that is either too big or too small for your usage patterns, allowing you to make changes that can save money in both situations.

How about folks who stop to buy those crazy coffees? You know what I'm talking about, the café-choco-frappo-latte that costs $5 a cup. Some people buy several of these coffees each day, which can add up to over $3,600 dollars a year. Instead of going to the coffee shop, how about buying the ingredients and making it at home? You might find out that you make a better cup of coffee, and you can save yourself $3,000 as well!

Here's a picture for you. It's Friday afternoon, payday for many, and you walk into a convenience store and there's somebody in front of you spending all kinds of money purchasing lottery and scratch tickets. They are hoping to hit it big, right? We discussed the lottery earlier, the odds of hitting the jackpot are 1 in 170 million. I get it when people buy $1 or maybe $2 dollars worth of lottery tickets, that's entertainment. But, if you're spending much of your paycheck on these tickets, thinking your life is about to change, you'll be right when your spouse finds out what you did with the grocery money!

The Income Tax Code in America is known as a progressive tax, the more income earned the higher one's tax rate. This structure of taxation was devised as a way to help redistribute wealth. Lottery tickets are just the opposite. Data suggests that purchasers of lottery and scratch tickets tend to have lower incomes, which means these tickets serve as a regressive tax. And, they are a tax, as proceeds go to fund state and local government programs. While you can't legally evade the income tax, you can evade the "lottery tax", by not buying them! Lotteries are the result of failed government fiscal policies, and financially penalize those that can least afford it.

If you want to avoid the lottery and scratch ticket tax, try thinking about the odds of hitting the jackpot, 1 in 170 million, and then compare that to the odds of the average individual having sex today, which is 2 in 7. Why would you waste time standing in line for a lottery ticket; you need to get home, now!

Another suggestion, go to your payroll department and ask them to set up direct deposit for your paycheck. That way you won't have excess cash in your pocket when you walk into a convenience store.

If you want to attract money, you need to respect it. Pick up the pennies you see on the street and remember that money is a means to an end, reaching a goal or destination. Sing the Aretha Franklin tune, R-E-S-P-E-C-T, and be aware of its evil cousin, G-R-E-E-D. Greed can lead to crime, and crime doesn't pay!

Wealth Building Task

Wealth Building Task Two: Reread your completed Chapter One assignment and review the list of things that you want to change. Now, write how you'll feel when you've eliminated each of your money concerns. For example, when I've paid off my credit card debt, I'll sleep better and likely perform better at my job. And this will put me in a better position for a promotion or a raise.

Note: If you didn't already upload your free "Wealth Building Task" book, go to www.philipspillane.com and you will find it under the Resource tab; save it to your computer.

Chapter 3

Take Inventory

"To state the facts frankly is not to despair the future nor indict the past.
The prudent heir takes careful inventory of his legacies
and gives faithful accounting to those whom he owes an obligation of
trust."
John F. Kennedy

You Don't Have to Be an Accountant

In this chapter you will learn to take a snapshot of your economic well being. After all, you have to know where you are starting from in order to build a plan that can help you achieve your destinations. Think of it this way, if you were driving a car to Los Angeles, wouldn't it make a difference, for planning purposes, to know if you were starting from Washington DC versus Kansas City? Of course it would, you would need an extra day to travel from Washington DC than you would from Kansas City. So, if you don't know where you are starting from regarding wealth, how can you properly build a plan that will allow you to reach your destinations, on time and without having to take undue risk? To help you with this we will create three simple statements:

1. Net Worth Statement,
2. Budget/Expense Statement, and
3. Income Statement.

John and/or Jane Doe
Personal Net Worth Statement

Assets (things you own)		Liabilities (What you owe)	
Cash on Hand	$75	Personal Loans	$0
Checking Account	$1,200	Student Loans	$0
Savings Account	$2,000	Credit Card Balance	$5,000
Money Market	$5,000	Auto Loans	$10,000
Certificate of Deposit	$0	Mortgage	$190,000
Personal Property	$20,000	Home Equity Loan	$0
Market Value of Your Home	$200,000	Past Due Taxes	$0
Other Real Estate	$0	Life Insurance Loans	$0
Non Retirement Investment Accounts	$20,000	Other Liabiliites	$0
Retirement Investment Accounts	$100,000		
Cash Value of Life Insurance	$0		
Other Assets	$0		
Total Assets	$348,275	Total Liabilities	$205,000
Personal Net Worth (Subtract Total Liabilities from Total Assets) $348,275 - $205,000 = $143,275			
Ex: Personal Property: Auto's, Furniture, Collectibles, other things you own			

The first statement identifies your Net Worth. It lists or itemizes your assets (things you own), and your liabilities (things you owe). When we subtract Total Liabilities from Total Assets we derive your Personal Net Worth. In the example you can see that John and/or Jane Doe have a Personal Net Worth of $143,275. The goal over time is to grow your Personal Net Worth. By completing the Net Worth Statement you can evaluate your success in building wealth. And, if you're really serious, you might update your Net Worth more frequently than once a year. Some people complete their Net Worth Statement monthly as a way to help them stay on course toward long term goals. Know that banks often request or require Net Worth Statements before lending individuals money, so by creating your own statement, and updating it regularly, you'll save time when you apply for a loan.

What if your Personal Net Worth ends up negative? While that's certainly not ideal, it does happen. Don't fret, we're going to discuss plenty of strategies to turn your Net Worth into a positive number.

The order in which you list your assets and liabilities really doesn't matter, but if you want to do it like an accountant, list the most liquid assets first, those that are either already in cash form or can easily be converted to cash. For instance, real estate isn't generally considered highly liquid. If you wanted to convert real estate to cash, you'd first have to list the property for sale, then find a buyer who might need time to arrange for financing, and eventually you complete the transaction at a real estate closing. Clearly, real estate is not a liquid asset. No matter what order you choose to list your Assets and Liabilities; the arithmetic will come out the same way when you total the columns.

It is a good idea, when creating or updating your Net Worth Statement, to write notes to yourself, on the statement, that can serve as reminders as to what you included in certain line items. For instance, if you had a line titled "Personal Property", your note would remind you of the things accounted for under this title, e.g. jewelry, clothing, etc.

Additional

Books

Available

at

www.amazon.com

www.barnesandnoble.com

zip ?

*I gave new copy to 6/30/14
Amelia Blmer
2895 Ethan Allen
, highway
Georgia, VT 05478
St. A*

Budget/Expense Statement				
	Budgeted Expenses	Actual Expenses	$ Under or Over Budget	% of Total Budget	Month End Notes
Food:					
Groceries	440	500	-60	16%	Lobster dinner
Other	NA	NA	NA		
Subtotals	**440**	**500**	**-60**	**16%**	
Housing:					
Mortgage/Rent	1000	1000		31%	
Maintenance	25	10	15	0%	
Other	NA	NA			
Subtotals	**1025**	**1010**	**15**	**31%**	
Utilities:					
Phone	60	70	-10	2%	International call
Cable	100	100		3%	
Internet	50	50		2%	
Propane/Natural Gas	NA	NA			
Electric	80	75	5	2%	
Heating Oil	NA	NA			
Water/Sewer	50	50		2%	
Trash/Recycling	30	30		1%	
Other	NA	NA			
Subtotals	**370**	**375**	**-5**	**12%**	
Transportation:					
Auto(s) loan/lease	200	200		6%	
Gas/Diesel	200	150	50	5%	Car pooled one week
Mass Transit	NA	NA			
Other	NA	NA			
Subtotals	**400**	**350**	**50**	**11%**	
Insurances:					
Home	50	50		2%	
Auto	80	80		2%	
Health	400	400		12%	
Life	20	20		0%	
Disability	NA	NA			
Other	NA	NA			
Subtotals	**550**	**550**		**16%**	
Personal:					
Student Loans	NA	NA			
Entertainment	100	150	-50	5%	Extra night out
Health Club	50	50		2%	
Clothing	200	175	25	5%	Bought on sale
Hair/Personal Care	50	50		2%	
Dry Cleaning	25	20	5	0%	
Licenses, Dues, Subscriptions	15	15		0%	
Medical Insurance	NA	NA			
Other	NA	NA			
Subtotals	**440**	**460**	**-20**	**14%**	
Grand Total	**$3,225**	**$3,245**	**-20**	**100%**	

The next statement is the Budget/Expense Statement, which identifies where you are spending money, and can be used to compare actual expenses to projected expenses. You will want to complete and review this statement monthly to identify budget over runs or where you may have spent less than expected, if you are so lucky. From this information you can ask yourself critical questions about your spending patterns, and use this information to build better budgets or spending strategies. With each successive monthly review, you will find it easier to project your budget, as well as build strategies to cut costs and save money that might eventually be invested for your future.

Reviewing the sample statement you will see that we have categorized expenses to make it easier to review. In the first column we list our projections or budget for the month, our goal. In the first few months of completing this statement, you might find it helpful to review past credit card bills, checking and debit account statements, as well as actual billing statements you received to build your budget. Eventually you'll be able to use previous month's statements to complete most of your budget estimates.

At the end of each month, you will then fill in actual expenditures in the second column, again using actual bills, check registers, and debit statements. To capture out-of-pocket spending, I recommend keeping a small note book with you and recording cash transactions as they occur; you'll be surprised how much you can spend out-of-pocket each month.

Next, subtract Actual Expenses from Budgeted Expenses to determine if you went over or under budget for the month, and insert this in the third column.

The fourth column gives us another way of analyzing expense data, by converting dollars spent per line item into percent of budget spent per line item. This is simple math; you divide each line item of Actual Expense by the Grand Total of Expenses.

Lastly, you will want to write notes to yourself in the final column to explain why you went over or under budget. I would focus your notes on areas that you were significantly over or under budget. These notes are a reminder of what is keeping you from achieving your ultimate goal of building wealth, or will help you understand what strategies are working well for you. They don't have to be elaborate, just something to hold you accountable for your budget!

As previously mentioned, your first few months of completing this statement are likely to be eye opening, especially when you look at cash transactions. You might be shocked at how much you're spending on things like that café-frappo-coffee drink, or lottery tickets, the things that might be keeping you from building true wealth!

Within the budgeting process you should begin thinking of strategies to reduce your expenses immediately. Here are a few ideas, but by no means is this to be considered a complete list. By the way, my wife is one of ten children, so some of these ideas are hers:

Groceries:

- Always have a grocery list of needs before entering a store, and stick to the list.
- Don't go shopping on an empty stomach, it leads to impulsive purchases.
- Use coupons from magazines or on the internet, but don't buy things just because you have a coupon.
- Substitute name brands for store brands, if they meet the taste test!

- Shop multiple stores based on promotions, you might buy meats at one store and produce at another.
- Consider shopping at "Club" stores if the membership fee can be paid by cost savings during the year.

Housing:
- This is a big ticket item, don't try to keep up with the Jones's.

Utilities:
- If you have an option, shop for providers and ask about special pricing programs. You might shop this area each year.
- Practice energy efficiency. Turn off lights when they are not needed. Turn your home heating back a few degrees and put on a sweater. Turn the air conditioner back and use shades to block the sun from heating the house. Take shorter showers.

Telecommunications:
- Don't upgrade your cell phone every time a new model is released. Review usage and determine the best data plan based on usage needs.
- Utilize bundled programs (Cell phone, Internet, Cable TV) but be aware of contract periods. Question the need to receive 100 TV stations, as well as the need for a 60 inch screen with surround sound.

Transportation:
- Use public transportation when possible. Buy fuel efficient automobiles, and don't trade cars frequently. Since cars are depreciating assets, consider driving them as long as they are safe, for 10 years or more. Try to pay for cars without financing. Who wants to pay interest on something that is losing value everyday?

Insurances:

- Life, home, and auto insurance are very competitive industries. Shop around and ask for discounts: Safe driver; good student; bundled programs (home and auto through the same company). Live a healthy lifestyle. Consider higher deductible allowances.

Personal:

Remember, I told you that I would tell you what you need to hear, not necessarily what you want to hear.

- Consider going to dinner at a less expensive restaurant. Buy knock off designer clothing.

This all comes down to deciding what you need versus what you want, and then living with your decisions. I have only brushed the surface of ways to save money and I know some of you probably have great strategies that we could all benefit from. Go to my web site, tell me about your budget saving strategies, and maybe we can share some of the best ideas on the site. www.philipspillane.com

John and/or Jane Doe
Income Statement

Projected Monthly Net Income		Projected Monthly Expenses	Projected Monthly Savings (Subtract Projected Monthly Expenses from Projected Total Net Income)
Job #1 $	$		
Job #2 $	$		
Job #3 $	$		
Total $	**$**	**$**	**$**
Actual Monthly Net Income		Actual Monthly Expenses	Actual Monthly Savings (Subtract Actual Expenses From Total Actual Income)
Job #1 $	$		
Job #2 $	$		
Job #3 $	$		
Total $	**$**	**$**	**$**

If Projected or Actual Savings is a Negative Number You Are Living Above Your Means i.e. Spending to Much!

Finally, let's discuss the Income Statement. You will see that we first list Projected Monthly Income from all job sources. Next we input Projected Expenses for the month, in column two, which comes directly off of our Expense Budget Statement. We then subtract Projected Expenses from Projected Income to determine if we will have a surplus (savings) or a short fall of funds for the month. If there is a shortfall, we need to consider cutting projected expenses or determine where funds will come from to cover the shortfall. Hint, the credit card isn't the answer!

At the end of the month, we can compare actual expenses to actual income, and if we have been successful with the budget process, we allocate savings to either a "rainy day" bank fund, or to long-term investment options.

For those salaried readers, completing the income portion of the Income Statement will be easy, but for hourly workers it may require additional planning. In either situation, this statement gives you the opportunity to think critically about income and expenses to help avoid that nasty four letter word, debt!

Wealth Building Task

Wealth Building Task Three: Complete a Net Worth Statement, Expense/ Budget Statement and Income Statement, for yourself. You can use the examples in the chapter to create your own format, or if you have already uploaded the free "Wealth Building Task" book from www.philipspillane. com, under the Resource tab, use the templates provided under Wealth Building Task Three. Take your time and don't move on to the next chapter until these statements are completed. If you need motivation at this point, re-read your Wealth Building Tasks from Chapter One, and read your Wealth Building Tasks responses in Chapter Two. I think you will find each time you update these statements they become easier to complete, than the previous time.

Chapter 4

Defining Your Destination

*"If you don't know where you're going,
you'll end up someplace else."*
Yogi Berra

What's Really Important to You?

In the last Chapter you learned to complete three important financial statements that help measure your financial well being. Now we want to move to where it is that you want to go, relative to building wealth. There was a Canadian philosopher, Marshall McCluen, who believed the problem with people is that we tend to drive forward while looking into our rearview mirror. Meaning we tend to look back and see the things we've done and the mistakes we've made, but we don't plan for where we want to go; that's what this chapter is all about. You are going to learn to look forward and define what's important to you, your destinations in life, and build a plan to achieve these destinations. This chapter is about the things you want that will require time, money and planning.

As a starting point for developing your goals and destinations, I would like you to consider a theory presented by Abraham Maslow in 1943, which he called "A Theory of Human Motivation". Maslow theorized that man is motivated at the initial level of his model to meet basic life requirements, such as food and water, before he is motivated to seek the next level of hierarchy, that of safety, shelter and employment. Following this, man becomes motivated to achieve love and a sense of belonging which is accomplished by creating friendships and families. At the fourth level, man is motivated to achieve self-esteem which provides confidence, winning awards and peer recognition. Finally, man is motivated to achieve self-actualization, which I define as "having arrived". This is the point in life where you have achieved everything that you have ever wanted and now you have the luxury of helping others. The reason I offer this theory is to help you understand where you might be in this hierarchy and where you would like to go. It will help you develop your destinations in life, what you are motivated to achieve!

SMAC

It's time to start thinking about setting goals that can be life altering, or game changers! To help you achieve your destinations I want you to establish your goals using a unique process that I have found incredibly effective and goes by the acronym "SMAC". SMAC stands for Specific, Measurable, Attainable and Compatible, criteria that all goals should meet. So let's look at what this means:

Specific: A specific goal is one that is clearly defined. Let's look at an example of a goal that is not specific: My goal is to be rich. Can anyone tell me the exact definition of being rich? No, this is a subjective term, meaning we all have a different interpretation of what rich is. For some, rich is having a million dollars, and for others it might be having tens of millions of dollars. So, our first step in setting goals is to learn to be very specific, objective versus subjective. Instead of saying "My goal is to be rich", lets try this, "I want a million dollars of investable assets at retirement, age 62, because I consider that rich." That's a pretty specific goal defined by both dollars and age, and it explains why the goal is important, to make the individual feel rich.

Measurable: Measureable goals are those that establish quantifiable criteria, such as time, dollars, etc. In our example above, we can measure the success of the goal because you either have $1 million dollars of investable assets at age 62 or you don't.

Attainable: Goals must be realistic. In the example, if the individual had $0 investable assets at age 61, it's probably not realistic to think you can build a portfolio of $1million in just one year. However, if you had more time and the ability to save and invest regularly, it might be an attainable goal.

Compatible: Lastly, goals must be compatible with the rest of your life. Working 20 hour days to achieve a goal might be possible, but not really compatible with maintaining your health, at least for most human beings. Likewise, having to break laws to achieve goals is clearly not considered compatible!

Let's look at a goal and determine if it passes the SMAC test: A 22 year old individual with a salaried income of $40,000, working in a job they love, determines they have the ability to save and invest $10,000 per year. They have a moderate risk tolerance, which we'll talk about in greater detail later, and they plan to work with a Certified Financial Planner ™, a professional that will help them allocate their investments into a Managed Moderate Portfolio of assets. The individual has a goal to build investable assets of $1 million dollars by the age of 62, at which point they anticipate they can generate $30,000 of income from the portfolio each year thereafter.

What do you think; does it meet the SMAC test? Sure, it's specific because it tells us the "what, when, and how". It's measurable because you either have $1 million at age 62 or you don't. I think it's attainable, based on a simple financial calculation that shows the portfolio only needs to return between 4-5% per year. By the way, returns generally can't be guaranteed; however, historical data suggest that this is a realistic return "potential". Finally, it appears compatible since it's a job they love.

Establishing goals is only the beginning, we also have to continually review our progress. This is where many people get off target, so to help avoid failures we are going to first set goals, next we will put our goals in writing, and then we're going to put these written goals in places where we'll see them each and every day. Why? Because people that set goals are more successful than those that don't. Those that set goals and put them in writing are more successful than those that only have goals in their head. And those that set goals, put them in writing, and review them regularly, are the most successful in terms of accomplishing goals.

Note that if you are a couple and beginning to establish goals, I suggest you initially write goals separately, then come together and review what's important to each of you. I'm not trying to start fights between couples, but you might find that you're not on the same page, and that's ok. Better to find out today that you need to compromise, than to wait until retirement and find out that you can't compromise. Always set your goals using SMAC, and make your goals ambitious.

Setting Your Destinations

The best goals are those that pass the SMAC test, because they help eliminate ambiguity. But remember that just because you used the SMAC process, it doesn't guarantee success. To help us improve the odds of attaining our destinations, we discussed the need to put them in writing, and then ensure that we review them regularly, staying focused on what's important to us.

As you begin focusing on building wealth and defining your destinations, I just want to mention that there are two types of wealth, monetary wealth that you can define using SMAC and that others can measure; and emotional wealth, which can only be measured by you. As an example, using Maslow's hierarchy, you might have a goal of providing shelter for your children, which is emotional wealth; however, if you already have a home, your goal might be to buy a larger more expensive home, which requires greater monetary wealth. The key is to set goals like destinations, which represent the things you most want to accomplish in your lifetime.

Keep in mind what Mary Kay Ash, founder of Mary Kay Cosmetics, says about goals, "A good goal is like a strenuous exercise, it makes you stretch."

Take a look at a sample goal sheet I call "Next 30 Years Destinations" and note if they fit SMAC, and cover both short and longer term goals.

Next 30 Years Destinations

Dated:

The following are the things that I most want to accomplish in life; they represent the destinations which require Time, Money and Planning. My Road map will help me stay on course to achieve these goals.

1. In the next 12 months I will eliminate all credit card debt, a total of $X. By eliminating this debt I will sleep better which will lead to better job performance, and perhaps a salary increase or promotion.

2. I want to provide my children with a good education, including college or trade school, and plan to pay for this education from savings. I anticipate the cost of this education to be $X, beginning in "Y" years.

3. I plan to retire in "Y" years and want to do so without any long term debt, including the elimination of my current mortgage of $X.

4. During retirement at age "Y" I plan to travel over the first ten years to each of the 30 states I have never visited. I project the cost for these trips will be $X per year, adjusted for inflation.

5. When I am no longer here, I want all of my assets to go to my children in the most tax efficient manner. Because my son/daughter is a spendthrift I want special provisions made to ensure they don't blow through the assets.

Your Road Map to Success

In Chapter Three you completed three personal financial statements to help get a picture of your financial health and now you've started to develop a picture of where you want to go and the things you want to achieve in your life time by using "Next 30 Years Destinations" goal sheet. Now we need to develop strategies to help achieve your dreams, and we do this by creating a, "Road Map to Success". It's your own how-to guide that chronologically outlines the things you need to do to make your Destinations happen. Harvard professor, Michael Porter, says a sound strategy starts with having the right goal. Writing "Next 30 Years Destinations" sets the goals, but completing a Road Map to Success, gives you the strategy to succeed. Take a look at a sample Road Map to Success and see how the Road Map chronologically lays out the tasks that you will need to complete to either attain your destinations, or to keep moving efficiently toward them. Once you complete a task on the Road map to Success, enter the completion date, which gives you a psychological victory, and motivates you to continue on your journey.

Road Map to Success

Date Completed	April-June 2013 Activities
	Update Income, Net Worth and Expense/Budget Sheet
	Interview and Select a Wealth Advisor
	Debt elimination review
	Review Next 30 Years Destinations

Date Completed	January-March 2013 Activities
1/1/2013	Update Income, Net Worth and Expense/Budget Sheet
1/5/2013	Review budget, and identify cuts to pay off credit card debt.
	Research and Interview potential Wealth Advisor
	Review Next 30 Years Destinations

Date Completed	July-Sept 2013
	Update Income, Net Worth and Expense/Budget Sheet
	Implement Mortgage Payoff Plan
	Implement Retirement Investment Plan
	Implement Education Investment Plan
	Review Next 30 Years Destinations

Date Completed	Oct-December 2013
	Update Income, Net Worth and Expense/Budget Sheet
	Complete Estate Planning Documents eg. Will/Trusts
	Review & Update Beneficiaries
	Review Next 30 Years Destinations
	Internet Research of States I Plan to Visit in Retirement

Trust the Process

Have you ever been at a New Year's party at 11:45 pm, and everybody starts to talk about what they're going to do in the New Year, that is establish their New Year resolution(s). If you're like most people, you never achieve your resolution. The most likely reason why you didn't achieve your resolution is that you had already forgotten it by the next morning. Yes, you could blame it on being hung-over, but the real reason was that you didn't write it down to remind yourself of what's important to you!

I want you to succeed, which requires you to trust this wealth building process. You will need to complete your own "Next 30 Years Destinations" and "Road Map to Success", and then put them where you can see them each and every day.

Here are a couple of ideas for locations to put these important documents: Put them:

- On your computer as the screen saver page;
- On your physical or electronic calendar; or
- Where you go a couple of times a day (no not the toilet, unless that works for you), on the mirror you look into as you get ready for the day and before you go to bed.

Again, why do we want to put our dreams where we can see them? Because it creates a repetitive act each time you read your goals and "repetitive acts lead to success." Those with clear goals are more successful than those without them; those with written goals are more likely to succeed than those without written goals; and those with written goals that are reviewed regularly, are the most successful. Reviewing written goals is like leaving your plasma TV on a static page, it burns the image onto your brain, allowing your subconscious to constantly be driving toward your goals.

Reading your goals each day is the mental practice that trains your subconscious. In Malcolm Gladwell's book, Outliers, he presents arguments that successful musicians, computer programmers, athletes, and business people alike were not necessarily born with special innate talents to make them successful. Instead an argument is made that these people simply put more time "practicing" their passions and careers, than did their peers. Remember, at the outset of this book I suggested that creating wealth is not a matter of luck; you have to put yourself in a position to "win", which is why we create and review our "Next 30 Years Destinations" and "Road Map to Success", on a daily basis. This concept isn't new, it's just presented slightly differently than what your grandparents and parents taught you, which is "Practice makes perfect"!

It's okay if you stumble following this process, just redefine perceived failures as successes. My friend Brian Cain, author of Mental Conditioning Manual, a must read book, helps some of the worlds top athletes get past stumbles. He teaches them to deal with perceived failures by saying things like, "No big deal," or "So what; next pitch," or my favorite, "Flush it"! I think you know what he's referring to when he says flush it. If you stumble, tell yourself the same things. In other words, don't dwell on the negative things in life, move on and pursue your dreams. I believe if you review your "Next 30 Years Destinations" and "Road Map to Success" forms daily, you put yourself in the best position to succeed. Just think about how you're going to feel when you accomplish your first "Destination". You'll be 100% ahead of where you are today.

Wealth Building Task

Wealth Building Task Four: It's time to complete your "Next 30 Years Destinations" goal(s). Use the example in the book as a guideline to get started. Next, create your "Road Map to Success"; outlining the things you need to do to help you achieve your destinations. Think deeply about what's most important to you and make sure your goals meet the SMAC (Specific, Measurable, Attainable, and Compatible) test.

Reminder: Free templates of the Next 30 Years Destinations and Road Map to Success are available to upload at www.philipspillane.com under the Resource Tab, look for Wealth Building Tasks Four.

Chapter 5

Miming the Wealthy

"Imitation is the sincerest form of flattery."
Charles Caleb Colton

Imitation

Have you ever noticed the influence that Madison Avenue, the advertising industry, and Hollywood have on us? For example, you pick up a magazine and see a model wearing a particularly sharp outfit, and you think, "Hey, if I were to buy that outfit, my life could be just like that model's." Or, how about when you see a popular actor or actress and they're sporting some bold new hairstyle, do you ever start to think that if you had that same hairstyle; you'd be just as cool as they are? Sure you have, otherwise the advertising industry would be out of business. We have all been influenced by various media formats that project images of clothing, hair-styles, cars, and more that make us want to be just like the characters seen in the commercial. They're darn good at it; we end up spending billions of dollars a year on items that maybe we don't even need. So, let me ask you this: If your goal is to build wealth, are you trying to look like someone with wealth? Do you mimic or mime the habits of the wealthy, and if not, should you?

Habits of the Wealthy

Put a mental picture in your head of what a wealthy individual looks like. Is your picture of someone that appears to be from Wall Street? They're well dressed and driving, or being driven, in a luxury car. Maybe they're wearing expensive jewelry or sailing on a yacht. How did you come to build that picture in your head, from TV, newspapers, or magazines? In other words, the media helped you build that picture from stories they covered, before. But that's not really what the wealthy look like. Sure there are wealthy people on Wall Street, but they represent a very small percentage of the true wealth in America.

If we want to get a clear picture of what the majority of "Millionaires" look like, in America read The Millionaire Next Door, by Thomas Stanley and William Danko. I was fortunate to have met William Danko, at a presentation he was giving on this book, and found that his research dealing with wealthy clients matched my own experience. The majority of wealthy individuals look nothing like your vision of a Wall Street Tycoon. In fact, you have probably walked past the "real wealthy" without having any idea of their affluence, and it's likely that some of them are your neighbors.

Lets review what wealthy people really look like, how they act, and their personal characteristics. First, many of them are entrepreneurs; they own their own business or businesses. Perhaps they are an electrician; plumber; own a trash service, small manufacturing firm, or even a fast food store. The common thread amongst them is that they are hard workers, putting in 70 and 80 hour work weeks early in their career, and taking very little vacation time. Eventually, as their businesses thrive, they tend to take more leisure time. These long hours of work support Gladwell's argument from the last chapter that success is driven more by time or practice than luck or some innate talent.

If you ever have a chance to talk with wealthy people about their early days in businesses, they smile and laugh and then tell you about the difficult times they might have endured in their business. You will start to wonder why they ever stuck it out. However, the more you talk with them, you will realize they stuck it out because they had a real passion for their profession.

I did, I do BUT...

✳

57

How do the "real" wealthy dress? Simple! They buy their clothes off the shelf, at a department store when the item is on sale. They don't wear designer clothing, unless you consider the logo of their business as "designer", e.g. Jim's Service Center. Their styles are often outdated, because they are busy building a business and seldom have time to read a fashion magazine. I remember an older neighbor that fit the "Millionaire" description. He wore neckties that were always out of fashion. If fashion called for a wide tie, he wore a skinny tie, and, when skinny ties were in fashion, he wore wide ties. Eventually I discovered that he bought his ties at a discount store, just as a fashion went out of date. He didn't care that his ties were dated, he didn't want to pay the price to be "in fashion".

What kind of car do the "real" wealthy drive? Once successful, they might buy a luxury car, but the vehicle they tend to drive on a daily basis is an older model car or truck. Early in my career I worked for an entrepreneur where the 80 year old CEO, worth an estimated $2 Billion dollars, drove to work in a 10 year old Cadillac. Your first thought might be, 'Why does someone so wealthy still go to work at the age of 80?' Answer: Because he had passion for the company he built! Well then, why drive a ten year old luxury car? Think back to Maslow's Hierarchy, I'm guessing that he was at the top of the pyramid and had reached self-actualization; he didn't need to have his ego stroked, he had achieved the things in life that were important to him; "he had arrived". He was also a bright man who recognized that cars are a depreciating asset. As long as the car drove safely, why trade it for a newer model?

What about the marital status of the "real" wealthy? They tend to have one spouse for life. Now, I understand divorce and death have a way of breaking up the one spouse lifestyle, but data suggests that those who have one spouse, versus multiple spouses, tend to be wealthier. The "real" wealthy tend not to be single parents. If you are a single parent, it doesn't mean that you can't build significant wealth, it just means that it's more difficult.

What about eating habits of the "real" wealthy? Sure they eat well, and they understand that meal time is a time to spend with family and friends. If they have a meal out, it's most likely at a home style family restaurant.

What are some other habits of the "real" wealthy? They respect their health and get between 7 and 8 hours of sleep per night. They don't drink to excess; they regularly exercise but that doesn't mean they're in a gym lifting weights, or running marathons. Instead they are out of doors kayaking, skiing, hiking, fishing, or hunting. It shouldn't come as a surprise, but the "real" wealthy are terrific savers, generally saving about 20% of their annual income. It might seem impossible for you to save 20% of your annual income now, but by embracing the things you are learning in this book, your goal should eventually be to save 20% of your income.

The last point I'd like to make about the "real' wealthy is their generous approach to philanthropy. We hear media reports about wealthy people, the so called "one percenters", described as cold curmudgeons that horde their wealth. But take a look around your community and you'll find buildings, theatres, parks, and athletic fields where the benefactor looked more like our description of the "real" wealthy than the one described by the media. The "real" wealthy are very philanthropic.

The "real" wealthy followed Ben Franklin's advice offered in his Poor Richard's Almanac:

"The way to wealth - have a good work ethic, be industrious and preserve; practice good stewardship of resources and be frugal. Avoid excess debt, be humble and charitable."

I'm guessing that recipe dates back to the birth of mankind.

Pick a Role Model

You now know what the "real" wealthy look like, and undoubtedly the characteristics described above brought to mind one of your neighbors or community members. Think about a time when you wanted to become a world-class athlete, a noted scientist, a big time banker, a world-class teacher, or maybe a renowned gourmet chef. It's likely that you had, or may have, someone in mind that would inspire you, a role model, to pursue these fields. If your goal is to build wealth, do you have a role model? If not, look around your community and find an individual that you either know personally, or someone that you can observe. Begin to notice their habits, their personal characteristics, and start emulating them. (Warning: Don't mime or emulate someone that is building wealth illegally.) As the saying goes, "If you want to fly with the eagles, you can't be a turkey."

Wealth Building Task

Wealth Building Task Five: Write down the name of your role model, and what characteristics they have, so that if you mimicked them; you could build your own wealth. Example: John Doe is my wealth role model. John works long and hard hours at his business; he paid cash for an older car that he drives, and he lives in the same modest home that he bought 30 years ago. He's friendly to everyone and he's humble.

Chapter 6

Build It

"The early bird catches the worm."
Proverb

In previous chapters we discussed strategies to minimize, and perhaps even eliminate, expenses using the budget process, a logical place to increase savings for your rainy day fund or to invest for long term wealth building. In this chapter, we will explore ways to increase income, and then we will look at strategies to allocate excess savings into investment opportunities.

First, let's discuss some ways to create and/or increase your personal income. Finding a quality job or earning a promotion, particularly during these past few years, has been difficult and requires more than a nice resume'. My personal belief is that too many people approach the process as though they are asking for a job or promotion. But you're not asking for a job or promotion, you're competing for it.

To successfully compete at anything requires setting a goal/destination SMAC (Specific, Measureable, Attainable, and Compatible), and supporting it with a clear strategy/road map.

So, assuming your goal is a specific job or promotion, let's spend our time discussing some common sense strategies you can use, sometimes called the referable traits. In Ken Blanchard's book, Raving Fans, he suggests that in order to stand out among your peers (competitors), you only have to differentiate yourself by one percent. That's right, differentiating yourself by one percent can earn the attention of those whom you want to take notice, employers and supervisors, and make them your "Raving Fans".

So, what are these strategies that can help you differentiate by one percent, and is it costly? The cost of differentiating is almost always $0.00. That's right, "nada", zero, a big goose egg! If it's so cheap, won't my competitors use them, too? Maybe a few will, but if it only takes one percent to differentiate yourself, it sounds like most of your competition is clueless about these strategies.

Here is an example of how a businessman made me a "Raving Fan", that is, he earned my business. A number of years ago, after working all week, I drove to our family cottage in Massachusetts to meet my wife and children who had spent the week at the shore. After driving five hours, I asked my son if he'd like to go for a swim before dinner, which he agreed to. On the walk back from our swim, my son innocently asked me if I was excited about the wedding we were to attend the next day. His words hit me like a brick in the head, and I stood for a moment in shock. I had completely forgotten about the wedding and had neglected to pack anything for the weekend except shorts, tee shirts, and a swimsuit!

Remembering how excited my wife had been about attending this wedding, I had my son swear not to tell her that I hadn't packed clothes for the wedding, "Let me break the bad news." I think my son rather enjoyed watching me squirm, waiting for just the right moment to break the bad news. Perhaps it was the glass of wine I served my wife, but when I broke the news, she didn't get mad. In fact, she laughed and suggested I ask neighbors if I might borrow a sport coat and slacks, but no one had clothes that would fit me. The backup plan was to get up early the next morning and go shopping for clothes.

Saturday morning I found a men's clothing store called "The Bay" in New Bedford, Massachusettes, owned by Tony Vieira. After explaining my predicament to Tony, he assured me that he could help. Within 30 minutes he had outfitted me from head to toe, with one small problem, both the slacks and sport coat needed significant alterations. I have shopped at many fine men's stores, but none of them ever provided same day alterations, and I needed these clothes within a few hours. You can imagine my skepticism when Tony promised that he would have the alterations completed in plenty of time for the wedding.

I figured I was going to have one pant leg or coat sleeve longer than the other. But Tony delivered, and the clothes looked great! He could have told me what 99% of other stores would have, that it was impossible to get same day alterations. But understanding my situation, he simply asked his tailor to put my alterations ahead of others that were not rush orders. What did that cost Tony? Nothing! What did Tony earn? He earned my word of mouth praise, which is the best form of advertising, and second, he earned my business. Even though his store, "The Bay", is five hours away from my year around home, many years later I still buy most of my business and casual attire from Tony.

Tony exemplified what I'm talking about when I describe referable traits. These traits are not hard to learn and it's likely that you learned of them years ago, but you either got out of the habit of using them, or you never believed in their power in the first place.

Let's review some of these referable traits:

- If you want somebody to do something for you, always use the word "please" along with your request, and mean it.

- Put a genuine smile on your face when talking to people, and look them in the eyes throughout your conversation. If somebody does something for you, thank them. Then send a handwritten thank you note. Sure, you could shoot a quick email or text a note, but taking time to send a handwritten note shows how much their efforts really meant to you. They won't forget a handwritten note! Always be on time for events, whether social or professional. A friend once told me about a business meeting that was held up because one of the attendees was late. Upon entering the meeting room, where six other attendees had been idly waiting, the

Always!

tardy individual stated, "Sorry I'm late; I was just being fashionably late." The supervisor of the meeting replied, "There is nothing fashionable about being late!" I'll bet that "little" incident damaged that person's career.

Why not make it a game for yourself to always be the first one to a scheduled event, it might just give you an opportunity to meet someone that you otherwise wouldn't have had the opportunity to meet, and could lead to a game changing moment for your career. Always remember, no one likes to be kept waiting!

- Display good manners. My mother used to tell me and my siblings, "Manners are something you can take with you anywhere, and they don't cost anything". We've discussed the importance of saying, please and thank you, but how about table manners. Picture the day you have a job interview scheduled over a meal. The last thing you want to do is exhibit poor table manners, because in an intimate setting like that, they will be noticed. I have been at meetings when the individual across the table from me didn't know the difference between a salad fork and a dinner fork, the butter knife from the meat knife. I've seen individuals leave their napkin neatly folded on the table throughout the meal. And, I've watched in horror as an individual chewed food with their mouth open, and answered questions while their mouth was full of food. I can tell you that instead of hearing what they had to say, my attention was on how ill mannered they were. I kept thinking of what an embarrassment they would be representing me and my company.

If you have questions about manners or want to be sure that you differentiate yourself by one percent, go online or go to the library, and pick up books by Ms. Emily Post. By the way, one college (High Point University in High Point, North Carolina) gets the importance of teaching students how to create Raving Fans. If you are a parent of a future college student, or you are a student looking for a comprehensive education, you should check out what the college President, Nido Qubein, and his team are doing.

As an example, the school has a steak house on campus where students can dine once a week at no additional cost. However, this isn't just any restaurant, the staff teach and remind students about appropriate manners. They have a sign at the entrance that informs guests that the restaurant is considered a "Learning Lab". Bravo, High Point University. Sure, they teach math and science like any other university, but they also understand that teaching, or reinforcing etiquette, manners, and respect can provide their students that crucial one percent when they interview for a career.

- Dress for success. Have you been to a wedding or funeral and seen attendees in jeans and tee shirts? Unless the invitation tells you to dress in a certain style, show respect to your hosts and dress appropriately. You don't have to buy the most expensive clothing, but don't wear what will put you in everyone's "loser" category.

Whether attending a wedding, job interview, or social event, here are a couple of simple suggestions to help you dress appropriately: When in doubt about the expected dress code, ask the host or hostess. If you can't ask someone, use good judgment and lean toward over dressing. You can always remove a neck-tie or suit/sport jacket if the event turns out to be more casual than anticipated.

I don't have recommendations for how women might handle being overdressed. But I can tell both genders, you won't make a negative impact being over dressed, but you will make a negative impression when you dress too informally. Think of dressing for events like a first date. Don't you want to make a great first impression? It's next to impossible to change someone's negative first impression.

Put yourself in a position to win a favorable impression of a new friend, new employer, or new supervisor. My mother always told me and my siblings, "Someone is always watching you and forming impressions about you, especially when you are not aware of it, so always put your best foot forward".

• Extend a proper greeting. When you are introduced to someone for the first time, you have an opportunity to differentiate yourself by one percent within five seconds. Put on a genuine smile, look that person in the eye, extend your hand to shake theirs, and grip their hand firmly. You don't want to crush their hand, but you sure don't want your hand to feel like "milk toast", a snack my grandfather used to eat, cold milk poured over a piece of toast. Got a mental picture of this dish after it has sat for ten minutes? You don't want your hand to feel like that toast!

Interviewing Skills

Interviewing skills should be something taught throughout all levels of education, but for most people, they are lucky if they even get it as a senior in college. After all, we are constantly interviewing/competing for something in life. In the early years it might be competing for a "privilege" like an extra piece of cake. As a teenager it might be competing for a date, and eventually you'll be competing for a job. The earlier we learn interviewing skills, the more time to practice and master them. Let's look at some skills and strategies you might want in your quiver.

Prepare for interviews. With today's social media, it's likely that you can find out a great deal about the person with whom you will be interviewing. You might discover that you share a similar background or interest, which you can genuinely incorporate into your interview to create a bond.

Use the library or internet to research the company you are interviewing with. Find out what the company's mission and vision statement are and then use that information to explain how your skills compliment what the company is trying to achieve.

Have a set of questions written out that you plan to ask the interviewer, and practice asking them. Stand in front of a mirror and ask your questions. You're going to feel funny the first time you do this, but this will give you visual feedback of how you'll appear to the interviewer. If you don't like what you see, or how you sound, the interviewer probably won't either, so keep practicing until you can say, "I'd hire me!" By the way, I suggest typing your questions; the interviewer will recognize you prepared for the meeting and didn't quickly scribble them while waiting for your interview.

Try and put yourself in the interviewers chair as you prepare your questions. Make your questions purposeful to help you decide if you really want a job with the company. Remember, an interview is simply a presentation, a conversation with a purpose, on the part of both parties. When you meet the interviewer, properly shake their hand and if you have a business card, present it. Make sure you have a couple of pens (that don't leak) so that you can take notes of the interviewer's presentation, as well as their answers to your questions.

Sell your skills and personal characteristics to the interviewer first, and then expect them to sell you the benefits of their company. Don't be cocky, but know that you are a valuable commodity, and if the job is a fit for both sides, it will happen.

At the end of any interview, put a smile on your face and genuinely thank the interviewer. Request a business card so that you can send them a handwritten thank you note for their time. Don't try to keep the interview going beyond the time the interviewer has granted you; this usually works against you.

If, after all of your work, you don't receive a job offer, you'll know that it wasn't because you didn't incorporate referable traits. Either the job wasn't a match, or you didn't provide them with enough information. Any time in life you hear the word "no", you should recognize it as simply a request for more information. Hey, I got a "no" from the interview, what information about me and my skills did I forget to tell the interviewer? Ahhh, I need to incorporate that information in my next interview. Don't beat yourself up if you don't get a job offer, follow Brian Cain's advice to top athletes, mentally flush it, and move on! Know that, "God don't make no junk!"

When you do earn a job, even if it's not your ideal job, be on time, and if possible get to work before your supervisor. You might get to work five minutes before the supervisor, but they might assume you've been there for hours. At the end of the day or week, ask your supervisor what more you can do for them, and be genuine; they'll read through any "BS"!

Learn from Thomas Jefferson's words, "I find the harder I work, the more luck I seem to have." Employing referable traits can put you in a position to achieve the kind of luck Mr. Jefferson was referring to!

Three Types of Money

In order to build wealth, you will need to have a clear understanding of the different types of money. I'm not talking about euros, pesos or dollars, I'm talking about types of money, based on their tax treatment. Once you understand the difference, you can build and implement strategies that will help you more efficiently reach your destinations, minimize your tax liabilities and maximize savings and investments.

The three types of money are:

- Taxable
- Tax Deferred, and
- Tax Free.

Taxable Income

Taxable money is the money you receive in the form of earned income. Uncle Sam created a tax code that says when you reach a certain amount of annual income they take a portion of that income to help pay for roads, bridges, national defense, and a whole lot of "pork" (wasteful spending). They don't really tell you they are going to use your money for "pork", they just do it! As you reach higher levels of earned income Uncle Sam, dressed in an IRS (Internal Revenue Service) suit, demands a larger percent of your income. We all need earned income, but it's the taxes that will kill you!

Tax Deferred Income

The second type of money is Tax-Deferred, money that can earn interest, dividends, or grow in general value without incurring a current tax liability. A word to the wise, the longer you can defer taxes, the more potential you have to grow your money. In other words, you get to use the money you might previously have sent to the IRS, as a tax, to invest or grow for your benefit. Someday in the future, when you withdraw these assets, you will be required to pay taxes, but the longer you can defer taxes; the more you might end up with, even after paying taxes.

So, how do you create tax-deferred money? You put money into a vehicle such as a Traditional IRA (Individual Retirement Account); 401k, 403b (Qualified Retirement Vehicle); or via an Insurance Annuity.

Tax Free Money

The third type of money, my personal favorite, is Tax Free money. The problem with Tax Free money is that there are not many places to find it, but a Roth IRA (if certain conditions are met to avoid being taxed), fits the description.

Understanding the three types of money is important, and you should know that they each have certain nuisances that may require you to get help implementing your strategies, either by working with a financial advisor or tax professional. The goal is to implement plans that minimize your total tax liability, efficiently using each of the three types of money and avoid paying incremental taxes. Stop! Read that last line again. You want to avoid paying incremental taxes, not evade paying taxes.

I'm simply telling you to use the tax code for all it's worth. By the way, the difference between avoiding and evading taxes might be 20 years behind bars, and I don't want anyone to go afoul of the tax code. My understanding is that the current tax code, written in 1913, started as a 400 page set of rules, and today it's over 73,000 pages.

Can you imagine running a business where your billing department had to understand 73,000 pages of rules? Perhaps that's why the federal government is running a $17 Trillion dollar deficit, that's $17,000,000,000,000.00, also known as seventeen thousand billion dollars!

Reading this book, and then implementing sound personal financial strategies, is intended to keep you from creating a mess like the one our government has created.

Wealth Building Task

Wealth Building Task Six: Create a list of referable traits you currently convey to others and another list of traits that you want to convey, that might help you reach your Next 30 Years Destinations. Example: I need to get to work early every day to show my boss that I am committed to my job. This might lead to greater job responsibilities and an increase in salary, allowing me to save and invest more to meet my retirement goals!

Next, go to your list of assets and label them as Taxable, Tax Deferred, or Tax Free.

Chapter 7

Taxes, Inflation & Compound Interest

"The avoidance of taxes is the only intellectual pursuit that still carries any reward."
John Maynard Keynes

Taxes

Now we need to shift and discuss three types of taxes: Income, Capital Gains, and Estate. Please know that you likely pay many other taxes such as Social Security, Medicare, Sales Tax, Property Tax and FCC Tax. (Look at your phone bill for a multitude of taxes.)

For our purposes we'll focus on just the following three:

- Income Tax
- Capital Gains Tax
- Estate Tax

Please note: I am not a tax professional, so for a more detailed discussion of the tax code, consult a tax professional CPA or Public Accountant.

Income Tax

The Income Tax, you will recall, is a tax on earned income. Earned income can include the money you receive for your labor, as well as interest received during the course of the year. Congress designed the U.S. Income Tax Code as a progressive tax, meaning the more earned income you generate, the higher your effective tax rate. The intent of this Progressive Tax versus a Regressive Tax (higher tax rates on lower earners), or a Flat Tax (same tax rate for everyone), was to redistribute wealth. That is, tax the wealthy more to keep the gap between the "Haves and Have Nots" close. Over the years, I guess an additional 72,600 pages of tax code has messed that up!

Capital Gains Tax

The second significant tax to understand is Capital Gains. This is a tax on the sale or exchange of a Capital Asset such as, Real Estate, Equipment, or Stocks and Bonds, to name a few. Note that the tax code views the sale of assets held less than a year as "Short Term" and generally treats gains as Income for tax purposes, whereas assets held more than one year receive special treatment known as "Long Term". When you sell a Long Term asset, it is generally taxed at rates below that of normal Income. Why? Congress, with the help of economists, wanted to give incentives for capital investments because they help the economy grow and create more jobs, which in turn can generate greater total tax revenue for the government.

Here's an example: Someone invests capital (money) in building a commercial real estate project (office building). The investment will help pay an architect for their design of the building and will pay a construction company to hire workers to build the project. The owner of the building will pay property taxes to the local government; the building will be filled by tenants (businesses), who hire employees that will pay income taxes. Tradesmen and tenants will shop and dine in the community, generating additional jobs and additional payroll taxes. Encouraging capital investments can potentially generate more total tax revenue than simply relying on Income Taxes alone.

Estate Tax

The third tax, perhaps the nastiest of all, is known as the Estate Tax also known as the Death Tax. Why do I call it the nastiest tax? Because, this is Uncle Sam coming after your money once you shed your mortal coil and are in the grave. Look at it this way, you work and pay income taxes, with the money left over you might invest it in a Capital project, which you will likely pay taxes on when you sell the project. However, if at the time of your death you have been successful enough, via your estate, you will have to pay additional Estate Tax.

As we move forward you will want to consider how each of the above taxes will affect you. With this knowledge, you can build strategies that utilize the most efficient monies available to you, Taxable, Tax-Deferred, and Tax-Free to help reach your life's destinations.

Remember, it is your legal right to build strategies that avoid paying certain taxes, but you cannot legally evade taxes. Before I move on, I know there are readers that will be incensed that I have suggested people employ "legal" strategies to minimize paying taxes to the government; they'll think I'm unpatriotic. If they feel that strongly about paying more taxes, they should go to the following web page: http://www.irs.gov/Businesses/Small-Businesses-&-Self-Employed/Where-to-Send-Your-Individual-Tax-Account-Balance-Due-Payments, and find the address, based on their filing state, where they can send a donation to the federal government. I'm certain checks will get cashed if they are made out to: US Treasury Department!

Inflation

The biggest enemy of building wealth in America are the limitations we place on ourselves; something over which we have full control. However, wealth building enemy number two is inflation, something that even kings couldn't control. So it's very important to understand what it is and how you can prepare for its effects.

Inflation is the general term used to describe the rising cost of goods and services. While moderate inflation of a few percent each year is generally considered okay, and represents economic growth, rampant double digit inflation seen in the 1980's, is a destroyer of wealth. If your retirement plan assumes that prices of goods and services (groceries, insurances, transportation, etc.) will remain stable throughout your retirement years, you're likely to be very disappointed and find your lifestyle forced to change to make financial ends meet.

How can you plan for something you don't control? You can use historical data to build certain assumptions of what inflation might be. Not just what it might be in retirement, but throughout your lifetime.

A helpful starting tool for a better understanding of inflation is the Rule of 72. Some of you might have learned it in school, but if not, here it is. If you divide the number 72 by a projected rate of inflation over a period of time, the answer will yield how many years before you need to have twice as much money as today, to buy the same basket of goods.

Let's look at an example, to clarify this concept. If I assume that inflation over the extended future is going to be 3%, 72 divided by 3 yields the number 24. This suggests that in 24 years it will take twice as much money, as it does today, to buy the same goods and services. If inflation was 4%, your expenses would be doubled in 18 years (72 divided by 4). Considering that the average retiree at normal retirement age is expected to live 20 years or more in retirement, you can imagine what problems inflation can generate if you haven't properly planned for it.

The Rule of 72 is not an exact tool since it is highly unlikely that inflation would remain constant over a long period of time, however, it is a useful tool to better understand the impact of inflation on your future budgets. You should use the Rule of 72 to help build financial strategies, but understand you'll need to be flexible and prepared to change your inflation assumptions from time to time. At this point you might be thinking, what's the point of planning at all if assumptions change? First, it's always better to be half right rather than not at all.

Those who don't plan at all have a much higher likelihood of running into financial distress than those that do plan. And secondly, you might find that the plan you designed, over projected inflation, which will provide you with excess wealth in retirement. Now wouldn't that be a fun problem to deal with?

So you know you have to take inflation into account, but you still don't know how much money you will need in 10, 20 or 30 years to achieve your life's destinations. Try asking yourself the "how much" question this way: If I/we were debt free today, how much money would I/we need to achieve my/our destinations, in today's dollars? (Present Value = PV)

Hmmm, if you haven't established being debt free at retirement on your Next 30 Years Destinations and Road Map, perhaps you should do it now. Next step, how many years away is the destination? (Time = n) What do I project inflation to be during this time period? (Inflation = i)? Using a financial calculator you could enter this data (PV, n, and i) and determine your future dollar needs. (Future Value = FV) That is how much money you need in the future, accounting for inflation.

Once your future dollar value is determined, you can build a savings/investment plan. I realize that most people: 1) Don't have a financial calculator, or 2) They don't understand the math. Hey, no big deal, I don't understand biology, or physiology, so I go to a doctor when I have questions. I'm not going to leave you hanging here, later we'll discuss ways to get the help you might need.

It is critical to understand how dangerous inflation is, especially if you don't account for it in your financial plan. Ask any retired person what financial advice they'd give a younger individual or couple today, and I'm certain they will tell you to start saving early and save often. They can tell you stories about what things used to cost compared to how much they cost now, never using the word "inflation", but that's what they are talking about. If you are fortunate enough to meet someone born in the 1920's or earlier, spend some time talking with them about finance; you can't help but learn some things!

Eighth Wonder of the World: Compound Interest

Our goal is to build strategies that help attain wealth, allowing us to achieve the destinations that are important to us. No conversation about wealth building is worth anything unless we fully understand the power of interest, particularly compound interest, as opposed to simple interest. Albert Einstein said:

"Compound interest is the eighth wonder of the world.

He, who understands it, earns it.

He who doesn't, pays it."

Let's explore the powers of compound interest by looking at an illustration comparing compound interest to simple interest.

Compound Interest vs. Simple Interest

In our example, we look at three different clients: Client A will invest $5,000 at the beginning of Year 1 and they'll earn 10% simple interest, over a 3 year timeframe. Client B will also invest $5,000 at the beginning of Year 1, but they'll earn 10% interest compounded annually, over the 3 years. Client C will also invest $5,000 at the beginning of the year, but they'll earn 10% interest compounded semi-annually, over the 3 year time horizon.

Following our illustration, you can see that Client A has earned $500 of interest at the end of year one and has an account worth a total of $5,500. In year 2 Client A earns another 10%, or $500, of interest off the original investment amount of $5,000, and now has $6,000 total. And, finally at end of Year 3, after earning $500 of interest, they have a total account value of $6,500.

Let's look at Client B, whose interest is compounded annually. At the end of Year 1 they have the same amount of money as Client A, $5,500. But at the beginning of Year 2, they start compounding the 10% on top of the $5,500, earning $550 dollars of interest giving them an account value of $6,050. Finally, in year 3 they earn $605 of interest and have a total account value of $6,655. The compounding effect has earned client B an additional $155 more than Client A, whose interest was not compounded.

If you want some real excitement, let's look at Client C. Their account is compounded at the same 10% rate as Client B, but it's going to occur twice as often.

Following the illustration, you can see that at the end of Year 3, Client C has an account value of $6,700.48. This is more than $200 above Client A, and about $45 more than client B.

Compound Interest versus Simple Interest

Client A invests $5000 at the beginning of year 1 and earns 10% Simple Interest over three years.
Client B invests $5000 at the beginning of year one and earns 10% interest compounded annually, over three years.
Client C invests $5000 at the beginning of year one and earns 10% interest compounded semi-annually, over three years.

A: $5000 at 10% Simple Interest

Year	
1	$5000.00 + ($5000.00 x .10) = $5500.00
2	$5500.00 + ($5000.00 x .10) = $6000.00
3	$6000.00 + ($5000.00 x .10) = $6500.00

B: $5000 at 10% Interest Compounded Annually

Year	
1	$5000.00 + ($5000.00 x .10) = $5500.00
2	$5500.00 + ($5500.00 x .10) =$6050.00
3	$6050.00 + ($6050.00 x .10) =$6655.00

Annual Compounding generates an incremental $155 versus Simple Interest

C: Let's look at $5000 invested at 10% interest compounded semiannually

Year		
1	1 st 6 months	$5000.00 + ($5000.00 x .05) = $5250.00
1	2nd 6 months	$5250.00 + ($5250.00 x .05) = $5512.50
2	1 st 6 months	$5512.50 + ($5512.50 x .05) = $5788.13
2	2nd 6 months	$5788.13 + ($5788.13 x .05)= $6077.53
3	1 st 6 months	$6077.53+ ($6077.53 x .05) = $6381.41
3	2nd 6 months	$6381.41+ ($6381.41 x .05) = $6700.48

Semi-annual Compounding generates an incremental $200.48 versus Simple Interest, and $45.48 versus Annual Compounding.

If you compounded daily at 10%, the ending value would be $6749.02, or an incremental $249.02 versus simple interest.

Now think about the possibilities if you made additional annual contributions and allowed the funds to compound over a 30-40 year period?

The value lesson offered here is that compound interest beats simple interest when rates and time are the same, and the more often compounding occurs the greater the return (semi-annual, quarterly, monthly, and <u>daily</u>).

Rereading Einstein's words above, you want to think about how you can use compound interest and growth to negate the effect of inflation; earn interest versus paying it.

Wealth Building Task

Wealth Building Task Seven: Review your most recent Federal and State Tax Return and write down at least two strategies you can implement this year, to legally reduce your Income Tax, both in the short term and long term. Hint: One of the strategies might be to contribute (more) to a tax free, or tax deferred, retirement plan (401k, 403b, Traditional or Roth IRA).

Make sure you add these strategies to your Road Map to Success.

Chapter 8

Savings and Investing

"The art is not in making money, but keeping it."
Proverb

Savings

Think of building wealth like building a pyramid. At the very bottom of your wealth pyramid you need to have a solid foundation. If you ask a builder what's the most critical part of a building, it's always going to be the foundation. The foundation of your wealth pyramid, for our purposes, is represented by savings, (cash, checking/savings, and money market assets). These are your highly liquid assets, the assets we use to pay bills throughout the course of the month. These assets stand ready to pay for unforeseen expenses (rainy day), like when the mechanic tells you that your car needs four new tires in order to pass inspection, or the contractor informs you that you need a new roof on your home. Ouch!

Think of this base level of wealth as safe money, understanding that you won't earn much interest on these funds, they are a protection against "Murphy's Law". Murphy's Law says that the day you need money for an emergency, is the day that your higher yielding investments are in the tank, a.k.a. toilet bowl. So, we knowingly give up some yield to have a strong foundation that can withstand most unforeseen expenses that might confront us!

The next logical question is, how much money do I need to keep in my wealth foundation? Well, if I could read the future I would tell you exactly, to the penny, how much you need, but since no one can predict the exact future; I'll offer some ideas. I think a prudent amount of money to keep in your wealth foundation is between 6 and 12 months of your income. That might sound like a lot of money to tie up in savings, but if you lost your job, like so many have in the past few years, having 6 to 12 months of savings set aside should allow you to stay current with bills, until you find another job. This could be the difference between keeping your home and having it foreclosed upon.

Do you have 6-12 months of safe money in savings? If not, here's a good time to go back and look at your current budget and see where you might cut additional expenses, or increase income, to create that sound wealth building foundation. You know that $5 a day café-latte-mocha-chaca? Maybe it's time to start making your own coffee, at home. Don't be shy with your budget pen, be critical of your spending habits and ask yourself if each of your daily/monthly expenses represent needs, or are some of them wants? You may need a car to get to work, but do you need the car you drive now or is it just the car you want? I'd like a Mercedes S550, and it's on my destinations list, but only after I have achieved other destinations represented by appreciating assets!

Think back to our chapter about miming the wealthy, remembering that one of their strategies has been to live beneath their means; you can do it too! They buy cars and drive them until the wheels nearly fall off, they live in homes for a long period of time, they're not constantly upgrading, they take non-glamorous vacations, and they don't buy all the toys to keep up with the Jones's. Go ahead and take a look at the assets you have and identify bad ones, for example cars, because they depreciate in value. Could you manage with a more cost efficient vehicle? Next, look at liabilities to identify the really bad ones, like credit card debt.

Credit card debt is usually at the root of most individual financial difficulties. It starts off with just one purchase that doesn't get paid for when the bill comes in. The next thing you know, you're the victim Albert Einstein described previously, you're paying compound interest! Before you know it, you're not even capable of paying the monthly interest charge, let alone the principle. If you want to build a solid foundation for wealth, get rid of credit card debt, now or as quickly as possible! If you have credit card debt, it might be wiser to pay that off before thinking about prepaying your mortgage expense. Why? First, your credit card interest is likely to be higher than your mortgage interest rate. Second, credit card debt is not tax deductible where as mortgage interest currently is. Credit card debt can destroy your credit rating, potentially leading to higher future borrowing cost, if you can get a loan at all. There is no good reason to maintain credit card debt, other than to swell the profits of the card issuer. So, if you do have credit card debt, get rid of it as soon as possible (ASAP), and then only use your credit card when you know that you have the funds to completely pay the bill, at the end of each month. You get my take on credit card debt--it will make you a slave to interest payments!

Be prudent and fiscally responsible, you can't print money like the government does. Go through your budget and begin building your foundation of wealth, saving 6-12 months of liquid assets, holding them in bank accounts (savings/checking, money market etc.).

Investing

Now, let's talk about investing; the portion of your wealth pyramid that sits above your foundation, and represents money that will help you achieve the destinations you have established! By the way, I'm sometimes asked if money that will be used for a down payment of a home should come from your safe money or from investments. If you plan to purchase real estate within as little as five years, it's generally advisable to save the down payment in your safe money accounts. Investing assumes a higher degree of risk to principal, therefore, it would be painful to have to liquidate an investment, for a down payment, when it's "in the toilet". Play it safe here, add the necessary down payment to your 6-12 months safe money; you'll sleep better knowing the funds will be there when you're ready to buy a home! Investment capital (money) should be considered long term money. I know the media sometimes shows clips of someone that made a "killing" using a strategy of rapid purchases and/or sales of stocks, bonds or derivatives (options), but that is not investing, it's "trading", or as I like to call it, legalized gambling. Most gamblers end up losing to the casinos, don't they? How many times has someone told you how they made a killing gambling at a casino? Funny how they never seem to tell you about all the times they've lost at gambling! It seems to me that very few casinos go out of business, which suggests that the house wins more than it loses. Of course there is always the possibility of losing money when you invest, but if you use a prudent long term strategy; the odds of success might be in your favor.

Time horizons are a critical component to investing. Generally, the shorter your investment time horizon, the more risk one assumes. For instance, pretend you purchased a stock just before some geopolitical event, where the currency of a country crashes in value. In the short run your investment might go down, until cooler more rational thinking prevails. But if you had a long term perspective, you might find that your investment would actually benefit from the geopolitical event. I like to think of it this way: In the short run investment markets are irrational, in the long run they're more rational, but investment markets are never perfectly rational. So, try to think long term as you build an investment portfolio.

I sometimes hear from individuals that they think the investment markets are rigged, and only those on the inside make money. Tell that to the millions of Americans that have been long term investors, putting money into retirement accounts for years. They've lived through the ups and downs, but the long term trend has benefited their creation of wealth. Understand that the markets are blind. They don't see your race, your creed, or your gender. Everyone has an equal chance to grow their assets by investing, but you need to be willing to educate yourself, or trust an advisor, if you don't have the desire or aptitude to invest yourself.

Why not just put your money into the bank, where it doesn't take a lot of investment knowledge? You might just do that if, after establishing your Next 30 Years Destinations, you decide the type of returns you can earn at a bank will be sufficient to achieve your goals. But look at current bank rates, then compare them to the current and historical inflation rates and you are likely to conclude that the dollars you leave long term in the bank are losing purchasing power due to inflation because the inflation rate is higher than the interest rates at the bank.

Nobody wants to lose money, which is why many people are afraid of investing. Most anyone can remember the massive loss in value in stocks and bonds during 2008, but many smart investors were patient and didn't panic, giving their investments time to recover from the losses. Whereas, many stock and bond holders, with a short term perspective, helped prove "Murphy's Law" correct, selling at the absolute worst time. You have to decide what you want, and then analyze what it might take to get to your goal. For most people, it will require investing in the broad investment markets, stocks, bonds, etc.

Perhaps President Franklin Delano Roosevelt's words can help:

"The only thing to fear is fear itself."

In the 1970's I watched a program called Wide World of Sports. Once a year they covered a cliff diving competition in Acapulco, Mexico. Divers jumped from a cliff at a height of 100+ feet, into a narrow body of water with depths from 6 to 16 feet, depending on the tide. Not only did the divers have to worry about making a "clean" dive from these heights, but they also had to time the dive to enter the water when it was at its maximum depth, or risk death or injury. I thought these people were nuts! But that's because I saw them diving from these heights, but never saw all of the preparation that they put into diving. For sure, they didn't one day wake up, climb to the top of the cliff, and dive. They started diving as children from perhaps 5 feet, then 10 feet, and progressively moved higher as their skills and preparation allowed them, until they were competent to jump from 100+ feet. Investing is similar to high diving. You must educate and prepare yourself, or chose a trusted advisor that will help guide you.

Here is an algebraic formula that I use to help people better understand the variables involved in investing:

$G = R \times T \times I$

- (G) is your goal in dollars,
- (R) is your risk tolerance (aggressive, moderate, conservative)
- (T) is your time horizon in years, (when you need the funds), and
- (I) represents, in dollars, how much you plan to invest.

If we understand any three of these variables, we can mathematically solve for the fourth. However, the solution for the fourth variable may prove incompatible with the other variables. Let's look at an example: You have a goal (G) of attaining $1 million dollars in 10 years (T), with a one- time investment of $200,000. Solving for the required rate of return we find that you would need to earn 15% a year. Earning 15% a year would likely require assuming significant risk. If you couldn't afford that type of risk, you would have to consider changing one, or several, of the variables. You could lower the goal so that the amount of risk you would assume is in line with your risk tolerance, you could make additional investments throughout the 10 year period, or it might be a change of multiple variables. I strongly suggest that you manage investments to your risk tolerance, rather than managing your risk tolerance to investment goals. In other words, don't take on more risk than you can safely assume. Those that neglect this warning are often described as pigs, and we know that pigs get slaughtered everyday!

How do you know what your risk tolerance is? Risk tolerance is quite subjective, compared to the other variables. It seems when the investment markets are doing well, people tend to believe they can tolerate more risk than when the markets are doing poorly. If you're trying to measure your own risk tolerance, start by asking yourself how much of a reduction in value of an investment you could withstand in a one month, six month, one year period, etc. If you're working with an advisor, they can administer both a risk tolerance questionnaire as well as spend time analyzing your past investment experiences and how you reacted to market moves. Understand that is not uncommon for individual risk tolerance responses to change, depending upon your current outlook about investment markets.

Perhaps the most flexible of the variables in my equation is time horizon. It's not uncommon, particularly after the 2008 market sell off, for people to maintain their goals and simply extend their time horizon to avoid assuming more risk in their investment portfolio.

There is an old expression regarding investment success that says, "It's time in the market, not market timing that leads to success." The next illustration shows the power of time in the market, which is what my mentor was trying to get me to understand so many years ago when he encouraged me to enroll in the company retirement savings plan.

This is a hypothetical situation showing two investors investing at a 10% interest rate.
Investor A starts investing $5,000 per year at age 18 and invests for only eight years until age 26.
Investor B begins investing at age 27 and invests $5,000 per year until age 65; a total of 39 years.

Age of investor	Investor A		Investor B	
	Investment Contribution	Year-end Value	Investment Contribution	Year-end Value
19	$5,000	$5,500	$0	$0
20	$5,000	$11,550	$0	$0
21	$5,000	$18,205	$0	$0
22	$5,000	$25,526	$0	$0
23	$5,000	$33,578	$0	$0
24	$5,000	$42,436	$0	$0
25	$5,000	$52,179	$0	$0
26	$5,000	$62,897	$0	$0
27	$0	$69,187	$5,000	$5,500
28	$0	$76,106	$5,000	$11,550
29	$0	$83,716	$5,000	$18,205
30	$0	$92,088	$5,000	$25,526
31	$0	$101,297	$5,000	$33,578
32	$0	$111,427	$5,000	$42,436
33	$0	$122,569	$5,000	$52,179
34	$0	$134,826	$5,000	$62,897
35	$0	$148,309	$5,000	$74,687
36	$0	$163,140	$5,000	$87,656
37	$0	$179,454	$5,000	$101,921
38	$0	$197,399	$5,000	$117,614
39	$0	$217,139	$5,000	$134,875
40	$0	$238,853	$5,000	$153,862
41	$0	$262,738	$5,000	$174,749
42	$0	$289,012	$5,000	$197,724
43	$0	$317,913	$5,000	$222,996
44	$0	$349,704	$5,000	$250,795
45	$0	$384,675	$5,000	$281,375
46	$0	$423,142	$5,000	$315,012
47	$0	$465,456	$5,000	$352,014
48	$0	$512,002	$5,000	$392,715
49	$0	$563,202	$5,000	$437,487
50	$0	$619,522	$5,000	$486,735
51	$0	$681,475	$5,000	$540,909
52	$0	$749,622	$5,000	$600,500
53	$0	$824,584	$5,000	$666,050
54	$0	$907,043	$5,000	$738,155
55	$0	$997,747	$5,000	$817,470
56	$0	$1,097,522	$5,000	$904,717
57	$0	$1,207,274	$5,000	$1,000,689
58	$0	$1,328,001	$5,000	$1,106,258
59	$0	$1,460,801	$5,000	$1,222,383
60	$0	$1,606,882	$5,000	$1,350,122
61	$0	$1,767,570	$5,000	$1,490,634
62	$0	$1,944,327	$5,000	$1,645,197
63	$0	$2,138,759	$5,000	$1,815,217
64	$0	$2,352,635	$5,000	$2,002,239
65	$0	$2,587,899	$5,000	$2,207,963
Total Dollars Invested	**$40,000**		**$195,000**	

In this illustration, we have two hypothetical investors that can earn a 10% return each year. Investor A starts investing $5,000 per year at the age of 18, and they do this for each of the first 8 years, to age 26, and then they stop investing. Investor B does nothing for the first 8 years and then begins investing $5,000 per year from age 27 to age 65. At the bottom of the illustration, we see Investor A has a total portfolio value that is $379,936 more than investor B, yet Investor A invested $155,000 less than Investor B. If we subtract each investor's contributions from total return and then compare Investor A to Investor B, we find that Investor A has earned $534,936 dollars more than Investor B. How is that possible? It's the result of compound interest over time. Investor A had more "time in the market" versus Investor B, even though Investor B contributed more money to the investment. The message here is, "Get started early and contribute often." If investor A had continued to invest $5,000 each year, through age 65, they would have accumulated nearly $5 million dollars.

In the 1950's a theory known as Modern Portfolio Theory (MPT) was presented and quickly became the basis for most investment planning. The theory illustrated the possibility of constructing portfolios that would maximize expected returns, based on the amount of risk an investor was willing to assume, using complex mathematical analysis. MPT utilizes valuation of securities (stocks, bonds, etc.) to determine what their expected returns should be in comparison to the broad market. Using this data, a portfolio manager can construct asset allocation models that theoretically maximize returns for any given level of risk. Therefore, investors can choose portfolios that align with their level of risk tolerance. In other words, why invest in a portfolio that has more potential risk than an investor can assume?

If MPT is such a good theory, why all the noise when the broad markets decline? Because most investors don't understand the theory, and they let greed dictate a more aggressive portfolio than they should assume. When the going is good, the investor smiles, but when bad times come, and they will, the investor is likely to lose more than they can afford to. So, the key to choosing a portfolio for any investor is first identifying their risk tolerance, and then choosing a portfolio allocation that matches their risk. The investor needs to understand the likely maximum and minimum returns of a portfolio, and not simply chase maximum returns, unless they have a very, very high level of risk.

A good advisor can help identify your risk level and then make appropriate suggestions regarding portfolio allocation and construction.

If you are still having trouble understanding portfolio asset allocation, try this analogy: Both my wife and I like chili; I like it really hot and spicy while my wife likes hers less spicy. Our chili dishes consist of the same ingredients, chili pepper, tomato's, beans etc., but mine has a higher concentration of chili peppers. You might say that my chili allocation is more aggressive than my wife's. Most investment portfolios consist of either, stocks, bonds, cash or some combination of these. Within each of these asset classes, you have some assets that are more risky than others. For instance, within the stock asset class we generally think of smaller companies as having more risk associated with them than larger companies. Why? Larger companies probably have more resources to carry them through rough economic times than small companies. With bonds, we generally view corporate bonds as having more risk than government bonds, because governments can generate incremental income, to pay bond interest and principle, simply by raising taxes! However, if an investor assumes more risk, they should expect greater potential returns. Using MPT, we can develop portfolios that have allocations to potentially maximize returns for any given level of risk one can assume.

When it comes to investing, make sure your portfolio doesn't have too much or too little "chili peppers" in it. Think of Goldilocks, you want your porridge just right!

This chapter might be where you are expecting me to define a bunch of financial terms, but someone else has already done that, so I'd rather point you to some free web sites for definitions:

- www.investor.gov
- www.finra.org

I will explain the difference between a common stock and a bond. Holding a stock gives you a partial share of ownership in a company. As an owner, you should expect to share in both the profits of the company (via stock appreciation and possibly dividends) and its losses (via declines in stock share prices). Should a company fail, you stand to lose 100% of your investment. On the other hand, a bond holder is simply a creditor, a lender. The bond you invest in is essentially an I.O.U. from a company, and it states what they will pay the investor, via interest, with some schedule of payments and a return of the face value of the investment, at some determined time. Should a company fail, while you are a bond holder, you would effectively get in line as a creditor and hope to recapture some of your investment as the company assets are liquidated. It will be important for you to learn additional terms, whether you invest on your own or work with an advisor. So, beyond the websites listed above, I recommend picking up financial magazines, found at most libraries, as well as reading investment newspapers. I also recommend reading The Intelligent Investor, by Benjamin Graham; Warren Buffett's mentor!

It is not unusual to have multiple investment portfolios, each representing a different goal. You will likely have an investment portfolio for your retirement goals, perhaps one for educational costs for children, and maybe one for a second home. I like to think of these separate portfolios as buckets. Each one defined by goals using SMAC.

The most important bucket is the retirement bucket. Why? There is no do over for building retirement savings. If you reach retirement and haven't saved appropriately, you will either have to go back to work, not a pleasant thought, or you'll have to reduce your standard of living, also not a pleasant thought. I'm afraid too many Americans are ill-prepared for their retirement years. A 2010 U.S. Department of Labor statistic says that less than half of Americans have calculated what they'll need in retirement. And, only 30% of private industry workers that have access to a defined contribution plan, such as a 401K retirement savings plan, are participating in them. If you're going to live 20 years in retirement, and haven't calculated how much money will be needed, nor started saving for this phase of life, you might end up with one or both of the not so pleasant options discussed above. Let's face it, when we retire we all expect it to be forever, that is for the rest of our lives; and inflation is likely to erode our purchasing power. So, everyone needs to have a retirement plan, and start investing/saving early to allow the benefits of compound interest.

Some people go through life thinking that their Social Security benefits will cover retirement costs, but Social Security was designed to keep Americans from living in poverty, it was not designed to be a retirement pension. With our government $17 trillion dollars in debt, you certainly can't expect them to come to your rescue. If you want to properly prepare for retirement, you must state your goals in Your Next 30 Years Destinations, and have a plan in your Road Map to keep you on track. Think about the advice of seniors, start saving early, and do it often. Mimic the wealthy and eventually save 20% of your income each year. And, once you establish your retirement investment/savings bucket, <u>don't touch it</u> until retirement. If you need a new car, find another way to finance it, otherwise you're robbing yourself of time and the benefits of compounding interest. Your retirement bucket is a need, not a want!

It's time to look at effective ways to help fill your retirement bucket. If your employer offers a retirement savings plan, such as a 401k, 403b, or Simple IRA (Individual Retirement Account), join it as soon as you are eligible. Most plans require you to be employed for a year before becoming eligible to participate. Often, these plans include some contribution by the employer for participating in the plan. Put another way, if your employer promised to contribute 2-3% of your current income into a retirement plan if you enroll, why wouldn't you? Beyond your employer's contributions, any monies that you contribute are considered pre-taxed dollars. That means the money will be removed from your income, and put into your retirement savings, before taxes are withheld, remember this is called tax-deferred money. Incidentally, some retirement programs now offer an after-tax contribution that grows money tax-free. My impression is that the younger you are, the better these programs look, so carefully consider this, if you are given an option, between pre and post tax retirement savings. In either case, when you contribute to your retirement savings programs, you are ultimately paying yourself for a future retirement benefit.

For those that might take offense to me issuing strategies that reduce the government's tax receipts, let me remind you that Congress writes and passes tax law; they created tax incentives to encourage people to save for retirement, hoping to avoid retirees from living in poverty during their golden years. These are simply some financial strategies that Congress created.

For individuals that don't have access to an employer sponsored plan, you may be eligible to contribute to a Traditional IRA (Individual Retirement Account) where you invest up to a dollar limit set by Congress, that may be made using pre-tax dollars and grown tax-deferred, as long as your annual income is less than the limit set by Congress. Consult a financial advisor or tax professional for qualification rules and limits. Likewise, you may be eligible to invest in a Roth IRA, which offers the potential to grow your money tax-free, again, consult a financial advisor or tax professional for qualification rules and limits. Roth IRAs are one of those rare places where you can create tax-free money, as long as you follow the rules.

After maximizing use of employer and individual tax advantaged retirement savings programs, you may need to establish non tax favored investment savings programs to meet and fill up your projected retirement savings bucket. If this is your most important savings bucket, and it likely is, it is imperative to establish your goal early, then use your Road Map to Success, and review and revise as needed. You don't want to wake up and start planning for retirement at age 62, not unless you're retirement start date is age 102!

When you do finally retire, be careful of moving your entire retirement savings bucket to cash. It might feel like the safe thing to do, but inflation is almost always present, and it could significantly reduce the purchasing power of your savings. You might treat your retirement savings bucket like a "maturing" cliff diver, no longer diving from 100+ feet, but still diving! Input from a qualified advisor can help you make appropriate investment changes to combat inflation, understanding your time horizon.

The second investment bucket for many is the one for educational cost (college or trade school). I'm currently in the pay-out phase of educational cost, so I can tell you from experience that you can't start saving soon enough. The annual cost of a college education has gone up by approximately 6-8% a year for many years. That's more than twice the rate of U.S. Core Inflation.

Using our Rule of 72, that means the cost of college education is doubling every 9 to 12 years. Put another way, if you have a newborn child today and college cost continues to rise at the present rate, it's possible that the cost of college will quadruple by the time your child graduates from high school, for example, it doubles in 9 years and then doubles again 9 years later, when the child is 18.

I have a hard time understanding why these costs have gone up so much, because they're still issuing the same Paul Samuelson Economics book that I studied, nearly forty years ago. If the information being taught hasn't changed, why has the price increased at the rates noted above?

Understanding the cost of education, let's discuss some savings strategies you may use: Several years ago Congress approved what is known as a 529 Plan. This plan allows you to invest funds, using after-tax dollars, that can grow tax deferred initially, and if the funds are used for qualified post secondary education costs, all investment gains are treated as tax-free. This is another of the few places to grow money tax-free; take advantage of it! Each state sponsors a plan of their own, however it's important to know that you can invest in the state that has the plan that best fits your needs, which may or may not be the state you reside in. Additionally, these funds can be spent in any state without losing the tax-free status, as long as the program meets the qualification guidelines outlined in the tax code, under Section 529; hence the plans name.

Prior to the 529 Plan, many people used to save for education using the Uniform Gifts to Minors Act (UGMA), because it allowed certain tax benefits; however, under UGMA rules, when the child turned the age of consent, 18 or 21, they became the legal owners of the funds, and if they chose to use the funds to buy a motorcycle and join a cult, they could. Properly structured, the child is only the beneficiary of a 529 Plan, not the owner; therefore, if they buy a motorcycle and join a cult, it's on their nickel! And, in case you were worried about the term beneficiary in the 529 Plan, you don't have to die, it just denotes who the funds are supposed to benefit.

Note, regarding 529 Plans, it's possible that an account is opened for a child that decides not to go on to a qualified post secondary education. If this should happen, the plan allows you to name another child as beneficiary, and you maintain ownership control of the account.

While there are many potential investment buckets, for example philanthropy, starting a business, etc., the final one I'll discuss is the one for a second home. As previously stated, the time horizon has to be at least five years if you plan to invest in volatile securities, otherwise these funds should be allocated to bank type instruments, Certificates of Deposit (CD), Money Market, etc. If your time horizon is greater than five years, carefully consider your risk tolerance, and allocate your portfolio accordingly.

Wealth Building Task

Wealth Building Task Eight: Go to the following web sites, www.investor.gov and www.finra.org   and begin familiarizing yourself with financial terms. You won't be tested on the information but it will help you avoid potential mistakes.

Next, save these web sites to your "Favorites" so that you can easily revisit them in the future and look up terms you are not familiar with.

Chapter 9

Financial Coaching

"A coach is someone who can give correction without causing resentment."
John Wooden

Coach or No Coach

At this point, I hope you realize that to achieve most destinations, you'll have to become more than a saver, you'll have to become an investor. With each investment bucket you establish, make sure you set goals using the SMAC process. Think about Modern Portfolio Theory, and develop portfolio allocations that give you the best opportunity to succeed, with the least amount of risk. Some of the risks associated with investing to consider are: Interest Rate, Credit, Geopolitical, and Longevity of Life, to name a few. Understand that being a successful investor requires more than getting a "hot" tip from a friend, or getting lucky picking a security, when you don't understand security valuation, or the principles of fundamental and technical analysis.

My wife and I used to occasionally go to a horse track for entertainment. We would have dinner and then place small (I mean really small) wagers on horses. I read everything the race program offered to help me handicap a horse's likelihood of success, while my wife bet on the horse with the "prettiest" colored blanket. If you're investing using my wife's strategy for picking winners, stop! If you're trying to achieve your life's destinations, the things that are most important to accomplish in your life time, you don't want to bet on your destinations, instead you want to invest, and that takes hard work and understanding. I want you to succeed in attaining your destinations.

This is gut check time. Ask yourself if you can REALLY afford to be a do-it-yourselfer, with something as important as this?

Consider this: From 1977 to 1990, a gentlemen by the name of Peter

Lynch ran a mutual fund portfolio at Fidelity Investments called the Magellan Fund. During that time Peter achieved an astronomical average rate of return on the fund of 29%; that was almost double what the Standard & Poor's 500 Index (S&P 500) returned. But Peter claims that most of the investors in this fund actually earned less than the S & P 500 index. How can that be?

First, most investors entered the fund after Peter had been managing it for a time, and thus missed some really good returns in the early years. Remember our compounding illustration and the benefits of getting in early?

Secondly, some investors jumped in and out of the fund, based on monthly portfolio performance. If the fund experienced a rough month some investors took money out of the fund, yet, by the time they got back into the fund they had missed some significant returns. They didn't understand one of Peter's tenets:

"The key to making money in stocks is not to get scared out of them."

I'll bet that many of the investors that hopped in and out of this mutual fund were "do it yourselfers". Sure, over the years, people have done well investing for themselves during the good times, those were the times that you could have thrown a dart at the stock page and done okay. However, there is usually a day of investment reckoning, where only a surgeon should be operating, and only a well trained/qualified advisor should be helping you invest! Understand there is no such thing as a free lunch; in the end you get what you pay for. Ask yourself if you are uniquely qualified to be making investment choices that will determine the success of your retirement savings goal, or where you can afford to send your child to school, or whether or not you can buy a second home? If you are still not sure about being a "do it yourselfer" or seeking professional help, take this quiz. You'll grade yourself, and its okay to use the computer to check your answers, but be honest when you hand out your final grade.

Here we go. Relative to investing and finance define the following terms:

- Alpha;
- Beta;
- Efficient frontier;
- Yield vs. total return;
- Market cycle;
- Growth stock;
- Value stock;
- Arbitrage; and finally,
- Black Scholes Model.

If: your shirt got a little damp during the quiz, you thought the first two terms had to do with a fraternity or sorority, you thought the efficient frontier had to do with the U.S Land Rush, or the last term was nautical in nature; I think you need a coach.

Probably 80% of you believe either you're not interested in, or are not capable of, being your own financial advisor. The other 20% feel you have the requisite skills to successfully invest on your own. Yet my experience suggests that less than 5% of you should be acting as your own financial advisor.

Why doesn't everyone have a coach, a financial planner and investment advisor? First, people hate to feel like they are giving up control. But if you use an advisor, you have the final say, you're still in complete control. The planner and advisor provide you suggestions and rationale, but you have the final decision. The second reason why people don't hire financial planners and advisors is fear of looking "stupid". Hmmm, how do you think you'll look or feel if you lose all of your money? I'm perfectly comfortable telling an auto mechanic that I don't know what a "drive train" is or how an engine works, we can't be experts at everything. Stop worrying about such nonsense. The final reason people choose to be "do it yourselfers" is that they don't want to pay someone for something that they think they can do. Seriously folks, you pay a mechanic to work on your car, you pay the hair dresser to fix your hair, you pay an accountant and/or attorney to give you advice, but you don't want to pay a financial advisor or wealth manager to help you achieve your financial destinations? Forget about fees and focus on net results, results that are in line with your goals (risk tolerance, time horizon and ability to save). I'll bet you never question the fees at your bank. Some of you probably think you pay no fees at a bank. But isn't the difference between what the bank pays you for interest, versus what they charge someone to borrow "your" money a fee? I think it is and that fee likely runs around 3%.

I know some investors that manage a piece of their own wealth, they sometimes tell me how they are outperforming their advisor and wonder why they need them. Upon analysis, what I usually discover is that they happened to buy securities that were in favor, but that their overall portfolio allocation is inconsistent with their risk tolerance. So the individual has a little success investing and then assumes it's easy to do. Well, during "bull markets" it may be, but bull markets eventually end. Most individual investors dig only as deep as a security's past performance (1, 3, 5, or 10 years), never believing that past performance is not an indicator of future success. They don't consider how a security will do throughout a full business cycle, from peak through trough and back to peak. And they don't understand that business cycles don't run in exactly 1, 3, 5, or 10 year periods. A full business cycle could run longer than ten years.

Let me give you an example of a "do it yourselfer" I met some years ago. He was in his 70's and wanted some feedback on his $750,000 investment portfolio. Before looking at it, I spent time asking him about his goals, time horizon, and risk tolerance, relative to the portfolio. As it turned out, his primary goal was to preserve his assets for the remainder of his life. In your 70's you have to think you don't have another 40 years to live, right? However, when I reviewed his portfolio, it was evident that it was not aligned with either his goal of preservation or his time horizon. His portfolio was 100% allocated into stocks of dot com companies, these were small start-up, internet related, companies. Many of the companies had yet to create a profit for themselves. When I told the investor that I thought the portfolio was inconsistent with his goal of preserving assets, he responded by saying he had no intention of changing anything in the portfolio, since he had enjoyed a 19% growth rate in the previous year. My first thought was why he wanted me to look at his portfolio if he had no plans to change it, anyway. Perhaps he felt the need to affirm his success. Needless to say, he didn't become a client, and shortly thereafter the so called "tech bubble" burst, and many of the dot com companies went bankrupt. Assuming the gentlemen didn't make any changes to his portfolio, because of his previous year's returns, I'm guessing he lost nearly all $750,000. This is a case of someone that seemed to time the market, saw a 19% return, and then thought investing was easy. Had he worked with me, or another qualified wealth manager, he would not have had a very large portion, if any, of his investments in dot com companies, given his goal of preservation. It's likely that he would not have earned a return of 19% the previous year; however, when the tech bubble burst, he would have had a portfolio allocation designed to preserve his assets, instead of the one he had. If you believe pigs get slaughtered, work with a coach that helps "protect your bacon"!

How do you identify a good coach? Start by visiting your official state website. You should find a link to your state's Banking and Securities Division, which likely has a list of all registered investment professionals, and where they are located in your state. Some states allow you to look up an advisor's record to see if they have had any client complaints or industry infractions. These state agencies are there to help protect you from unethical practices, use their resources. Another website to visit is www.finra.org/brokeragecheck (Financial Industry Regulatory Authority), which is the regulatory body that oversees broker dealers and their representatives. Also check out www.cfp.org, the official site of the Certified Financial Planning Organization. You can see who holds The CFP® designation, where they are located, and if they've had any disciplinary actions taken against them. You can certainly ask friends and colleagues about advisors that they may be working with, but be very careful, the advisor might be nothing more than somebody's drinking buddy or great uncle. Things to beware of during your search include designations that sound important but lack any real substance. States and regulators are getting better at educating the public about phony designations. The state of Vermont actually lists commonly used and recognized designations and even provides a brief description about the designation. For instance, holders of the Certified Financial Planner™ Professional designation have completed a rigorous 2-3 year program including course work, a comprehensive two day exam, a minimum of three years industry experience, and requires ongoing continuing education.

Once you have identified someone as a potential advisor, call them and ask for a no fee meeting, where you can both decide if you want to establish a client-advisor relationship. At such a meeting you should be prepared with questions pertinent to your situation. You want to know if they have experience working in the areas that are important to you, for example, financial planning, investment advice, insurance, estate planning, etc. They should be capable of describing their practice, including their process, and they should disclose their compensation structure to you. You will be presented with a stack of documents, written in legalese that discloses data about the advisor and their practice. Don't let these forms scare you, they are designed to protect you and they are a requirement of the industry. At the end of the day, you want to know if the prospective advisor is truly caring (Do they see you as a client or a customer?), are they trustworthy (Do they have a good reputation?) and, (Are they an expert in the area for which you plan to hire them?)

Since I mentioned preparing questions for potential advisors, here are a few you might want to ask:

1) Are you a fiduciary? A fiduciary is someone that will do what's in the best interest of the client, putting your needs and interests ahead of their own. It is very important to understand this definition, because not all advisors act as fiduciaries. Many only follow the industry "suitability standard", which says, they will give you financial advice that they think is merely suitable for you.

2) Which industry designation(s) and licenses do you hold? Some levels of licensing prohibit the representative from selling certain securities. For instance the holder of a Series 6 license, under FINRA (Financial Industry Regulatory Authority), can't sell or advise you on individual securities (stocks and bonds).

If you already own such securities, this might present a problem. Make sure you know what the representative or advisors limitations are before establishing a professional relationship.

3) What is your investment planning and advisory process? If they can't give you a clear and concise description of their process, (what they do, how and when they will communicate with you, compensation structure, etc.), you might want to find somebody else.

4) What differentiates you, the advisor, from others in your field? What you're looking for here is their investment philosophy. If they just talk about making you "lots of money" before they know your goals, risk tolerance, and time horizon, be very wary.

5) How are you compensated? Are they paid a fee (hourly or a percentage of the assets being managed), or are they paid a commission, and how much is it? Remember there are no free lunches, advisors and wealth managers deserve to be paid. Look at net results, and be realistic in expectations; if you are in a conservative portfolio, don't expect the same potential returns that an aggressive portfolio might earn.

6) Can you describe your typical client? Does this individual work with people like you that have similar needs? If not, they may not be able to give you the advice you need.

7) If we were to meet one year from now Mr. or Ms. Advisor, what would have to happen in our relationship for you to consider it a successful relationship? If they come back with an answer that only deals with delivering high returns and doesn't address your goal and risk tolerance, relative to your time horizon, you may want to start a new search.

After interviewing prospective advisors, when in doubt, I suggest the "belly test"; you know, how does your belly feel? If it doesn't feel right, move on, interview more people. However, if after interviewing a large number of prospective advisors you always get that bad feeling in your belly, you might have an issue with trust, and you're going to need to trust somebody, sometime.

Finally, know that a good financial coach should help you clarify your goals, understand just how much money you're likely to need for retirement, and/or how much money you'll need for educational costs. They should build a strategy with you, and then implement and monitor your plan, adjusting as needed, helping you toward your destinations. They should also act as your quarterback in coordinating risk management and estate planning strategies, to be discussed in the next chapter.

Finally, a good financial coach/advisor will hold your hands when the water gets rough, and help you stay on course.

Sudden Money

"I am the entertainer the idol of my age; I make all kinds of money when I go on the stage. Ah, you've seen me in the papers, I've been in the magazines, but if I go cold I won't get sold, I'll get put in the back in the discount rack, like another can of beans". Billy Joel Lyrics "The Entertainer"

Congratulations you hit it out of the park or just inherited the mother load. You're an athlete, musician, actor, entertainer, or regular Joe, that suddenly has more money than you ever imagined. Now you can buy a fleet of expensive cars; a 20,000 square foot mansion for your mother; your friends now call themselves your posse; and, overnight you have relatives that you never knew you had.

Stop! Do not pass go, do not "spend" $200. It takes most people forty years of hard work to potentially reach a position of financial wealth where they can retire, yet you think you are there at the ripe young age of 22, 23, 24 years old. You haven't learned how to manage money balancing a family budget, or running a business. But it feels like you can buy the world and your dreams will last forever; and they might, if you step back and use your coconut aka common sense.

The world is full of once wealthy athletes, musicians, actors, entertainers, or regular Joe's. What makes you think you're different than them? They thought the Merry Go Round would go on forever, too. If you are a professional athlete your playing career is likely to last no more than five years. It took you 22 years to reach your pay day, and it's over in five years or less? You write and sing a hit song that sells a million copies, then incur "writers block" or lose your vocal chords from singing the hit song too many times. Your face was fresh in that hit movie or TV show, but your audience is fickle and wants someone new.

Eminen sang, "You only got one shot do not miss your chance to blow this opportunity comes once in a lifetime yo", in "Lose Yourself". So, you need to take care of your wealth, hoping that your career will last many, many years, but financially planning for the "what if it doesn't scenario". You need to be as disciplined with your new money as you were preparing for your pay day. That means doing without today, to put you in a position to have the things that require money, for a lifetime.

The single biggest mistake your predecessors have made is not having a plan developed and implemented by a trusted financial advisor. They needed a person professionally trained as a financial planner and investment advisor. Not their father, brother, or posse, or friend of a friend of a friend, whom may have had good intentions, but lacked the education and experience to guide them appropriately.

You will want a strong advisor that will say "no" to you when appropriate. And you will need to listen to them. If you follow the steps previously discussed in terms of finding a financial planner and investment advisor, I'm confident you can identify someone that you can trust, that is caring, and that is an expert. Once you have identified that person, it is very appropriate for you to ask the why questions, such as, "why are we investing this way', or, "why can't I buy another Mercedes S550"?

If you have done your job of identifying a good advisor, they will answer your questions equating them to your goals i.e. destinations. But, you will need to be prepared for, and accept, the "no" answer! "No, you can't have more money to take your posse on the road, because the cost will impact your long term plan in a negative way, which could mean you have to live at a lower standard of living than you said you wanted to during retirement".

If you understand that their saying "no" really means that they love you and that they only want the best for you e.g. to attain your lives destinations, I don't think you'll have to worry about becoming another sad story about the man or woman that had it all and lost it! Think of the 10,000 hours it's taken you to get here and hire a good financial coach. Retirement should be forever, and starting over would be no fun at all!

Wealth Building Task

Wealth Building Task Nine: If you don't currently have a wealth coach or financial advisor, start the search process. Some places to start your search might include the following web sites: www.finra.org, your state web site under Banking & Securities, and www.cfp.net. Once you begin interviewing potential advisors take your time, don't be intimated, make sure you feel very comfortable and that they are caring, trusted and an expert in the field, then make your decision on who you want to work with.

Chapter 10

Protect and Pass It

"Risk comes from not knowing what you're doing."
Warren Buffett

Risk Management

Risk management is the process of analyzing the probability of incurring a financial loss as a result of some peril (death, fire, theft, etc.), and then building a personal strategy to protect yourself, usually employing insurance. There are many categories of insurance; however, for the purposes of this book we'll focus on the categories I believe are most pertinent. Your job will be analyzing your insurance needs, perhaps with your advisor, and then building and implementing a strategy to minimize the risk of financial loss. As you build your risk management strategy, you'll consider employer provided options, as well as personal options where you retain ownership control.

We have been told that there are two certainties, death and taxes, so the first category we'll discuss is Life Insurance. It's understood that income producers represent an economic value to their dependents. Early in life your income is used to provide only for yourself. However, once we marry, and perhaps have children, that income creates a financial dependency for those we love. If you were to die, while these people were dependent on that income, it would create an economic and emotional hardship. Therefore, we consider insuring our lives, to financially protect dependents.

The question generally, is how much Life Insurance Death Benefit will dependents need, a very subjective question. We can project our lifetime economic value, that is our lifetime income. For example, suppose you could project that between now and retirement you could earn $1 million. If you were to die today, your dependents would lose the benefits that $1 million would have provided, suggesting you purchase a Life Insurance policy with $1 million of Death Benefit for your dependents. Another approach is projecting the financial needs of dependents to a particular age. You would consider specific costs such as, food, shelter, clothing, education, etc., and then purchase a policy that would cover those costs. Either strategy requires subjective thinking, and could benefit from an objective view of a financial coach.

Broadly speaking, there are two types of Life Insurance to consider, Term and Permanent. Term insurance is usually much more affordable than permanent and allows you to buy coverage based on a specified time frame: 5, 10, 20, or 30 years. This insurance can be appropriate in situations where you want to provide a benefit while dependents are young, or until they reach a specific age. Permanent Insurance is maintained, kept in force via premium payments, for the life of the insured, even if they live into their nineties. Why might someone want to be insured even when dependents are self-supporting? You might want it to protect a spouse financially; leave a financial legacy for children and grandchildren, or to provide a benefit for a philanthropy, Alma mater, art center, etc. Unlike the term policy, permanent insurance can build cash value, it holds monetary value while you are alive. If you reach a point in life that you decide you don't need the insurance any longer, you have an option to surrender it for cash value, however, there may be tax implications to consider. Just know that permanent insurance is generally much more costly than term, simply because the insurance company is assuming a greater risk of paying out a death benefit than they would on a policy with a term limit.

Another risk of income disruption is due to disability, partial or complete, where an individual is incapable of working. Depending upon the industry in which one works, or the hobbies they have, you probably have a higher chance of disability during normal working ages than you do of dying in this time period. Therefore, you should consider Disability Insurance (DI), which can cover lost income for both short and longer time periods. Please note that some Disability Policies cover only work related injuries, and usually covers only a portion of your income, usually 60%, versus 100%. After all, if insurers paid 100% of income, what's the incentive for the insured to go back to work? Additionally, some DI policies recognize that your disability prohibits you from doing your previous job, but benefits might be eliminated once you're capable of performing the duties of another job. Careful consideration is required to ensure that you purchase a policy that would meet your needs, in the event of a disability.

Like education, health care costs have sky rocketed, which in turn has driven the cost of Health Insurance through the roof. Without Health Insurance, you run the risk of financial ruin. Imagine not having Health Insurance and being diagnosed with a significant illness, or becoming seriously injured in a car accident. Medical bills can easily amount to hundreds of thousands of dollars in these situations. One strategy to minimize the cost of Health Insurance is to consider utilizing a policy with a high deductible limit. This means you are financially responsible for paying medical costs up to the deductible limit, and then the insurance company assumes cost beyond that level. In effect a high deductible policy is a strategy to protect against catastrophic illness, and can be a sound approach for healthy individuals or those that live a healthy life style.

Some employers offer Life, Disability, and Health Insurance, at a group rate, meaning less expensive than an individual policy, and the insurance is generally issued without going through individual underwriting, that is they don't look at your specific health condition. However, it sometimes makes sense to own your own individual policies to protect against the situation where you sever employment. Murphy's Law suggests that the day you stop working for a company, and lose your insurance, is the day you have a medical event. If you own your own policies, you don't have to worry about losing insurance simply because you change jobs. However, the downside of owning your own policies may be the additional expense, and the likelihood of individual underwriting.

Property and Casualty Insurance policies are designed to protect things such as your home or your car. Usually, mortgage companies and banks require you to maintain insurance on your home as long as they are owed money. Protection might include fire, damage from wind, water, as well as from theft. These policies can be like going through a cafeteria line, allowing you to pick and choose the things that you want protected. It is in your best interest to shop around, two companies insuring the same thing(s) are not guaranteed to cost the policy holder the same amount. An example might be an insurer that offers credit toward the policy premium for living next to a fire hydrant, or they may issue a credit for having an operational security system in place. You are likely to pay higher Home Owners Insurance premiums for having a dog, a trampoline, or a multilevel home where fire fighting would be more difficult. Shop around and ask your insurance agent to carefully explain your options. If you don't own a home but instead rent, you should consider Renters Insurance to protect against things like burglary, or water and fire damage to personal property.

In most states you are required to maintain Auto Insurance, whether you owe the bank money for your car or not. This is to protect other drivers and their property against damage caused by you. Again, shop around for discounts. Age and sex matters to auto insurers. Go figure. Young male drivers have a higher incident of accidents; therefore, their insurance premiums will be higher than their female counterparts. Interestingly, around the age of 50, if you have a good driving record, you might get a discount, but then when you reach approximately 65, your insurance premiums go back up, no matter how good your driving record. This has to do with historical data suggesting we begin to lose some of our driving skills around age 65. The more risk the insurer perceives, the higher the insurance premiums. Your best bet is to: drive defensively, stay out of accidents, avoid traffic tickets, and drive an older or less costly car (the insurer is thinking about the cost of replacement). Go back and take a safe driver course and get good grades if you are in school, many insurers give discounts for honor roll students. Keep in mind, like Health Care Insurance, Property and Casualty Insurance Policies do offer deductible limits. If you can afford to cover costs for damages, up to your deductible limit, it might make sense to purchase policies with a high limit, thus reducing your premium costs.

Finally, let's consider the risk of living a long life where special assistance, long-term care, might be needed. With the advent of penicillin in the late 1920's, medicine has made fantastic strides in battling all kinds of illnesses, thus increasing life expectancy dramatically. However, simply living longer doesn't necessarily mean living better. While today we might defeat illnesses such as pneumonia, using antibiotics, we haven't yet figured out how to stop the aging process of the body. As we live longer, we also increase the likelihood that at some stage of life, we'll need assistance/care to conduct normal activities of daily living (ADL) such as personal hygiene, getting out of bed or a chair, dressing, eating, and let's say potty management! You may have family members that are willing to provide this care, but understand that their noble efforts will come at some emotional and physical cost to them. Therefore, many people consider insuring the cost of potential "elder" care using Long Term Care Insurance (LTCI). These policies allow you to pick and chose the benefits that you want, however, they are fairly expensive and may have certain limitations, such as the type of care provider and/or facility you must use. Reviewing your options, you could buy insurance, opt not to purchase LTCI (taking financial risk), or assume that government programs like Medicaid will provide for you. You might have guessed, the government option is the least desirable, because you lose full control of your destiny. In other words, you might have to be moved to a care facility away from family and friends at a point in your life when having them nearby would make a tremendous difference in your emotional health. LTCI is a tough financial and emotional decision, which should be considered beginning around age 50. Know that the drivers of premium costs for LTCI are age and health, and the health curve seems to move against us around this age.

Legacy Planning

Legacy planning entails building plans and strategies to pass your estate to those you chose, at your death, in an efficient manner. If you don't properly draft a plan for disposing your estate, the government will do it for you, but most likely not the way you would have wanted. Let's review estate planning options that keep you in control, especially when you're in the grave pushing up daises.

The first document to consider is a Durable Power of Attorney. This document can be broad or specific, but it appoints someone to legally act on your behalf should you become incapacitated or unable to conduct business for yourself. In many situations your spouse can act on your behalf, but what if you're single or your spouse is unable to act for you? Imagine being incapacitated and no one is capable of paying your bills, such as home heating oil. If you live in the northern parts of America you know what happens when pipes freeze, they burst and cause massive amounts of property damage. By appointing a Power of Attorney, you give that individual the right to act on your behalf; in this case, to pay the oil bill from your checking account.

Can't you just put your children on your bank accounts, as joint owners, so they have access to funds if you are incapacitated? Question: Is it possible your child could ever be sued, perhaps for divorce? If that were to happen the courts might consider half of your checking account as your child's asset, meaning it could end up with that son or daughter in-law that you never liked in the first place. That's terrible to think about, so why take a chance? Eliminate stress, put a Durable Power of Attorney document in place at once. By the way, I know you can purchase these forms online, rather than having them drafted by an attorney, but, I wouldn't want to take a chance that it is written incorrectly for your jurisdiction. My advice, don't be cheap here, hire a professional, a lawyer, to help you with this important matter.

Create a Last Will and Testament for yourself, and file it with the appropriate probate court. This document should clearly illustrate to the court how and to whom you want your assets to be distributed upon your death. Understand that even with a Will it may take months for the probate court to approve and allow the assets to be distributed. Without a Will, the courts determine to whom assets are distributed, usually based on state law. Like the Power of Attorney, my recommendation is to work with a lawyer, competent in estate planning, so that the outcome is what you would have wished, versus having that no good son or daughter-in-law getting anything.

Upon your death, the Executor (male) or Executrix (female), named in your Last Will and Testament, begins the process of settling your estate. They ensure that all bills are paid from the estate, and provide the court with any information that they request. Once the court is satisfied that the estate is in order, they will instruct the Executor/Executrix to distribute final assets, and then the court closes the estate.

Sometimes individuals need more than a "Simple" Will to accomplish their wishes, so they establish a Trust. There are many types of Trusts, each designed to meet a specific need, like minimize estate taxes, provide greater asset protection from law suits, provide income for a spouse or special needs child, or perhaps provide for a charity. An Estate Attorney can advise you if a Trust is appropriate for your situation.

Medical Directives are documents that tell medical providers what type of care you want, when death is imminent. Without this document the medical world will attempt to keep you alive for as long as possible. If you think about the millions of dollars spent on medical care in the last few months of life, even though death is still the end result, you may want to complete a Medical Directive. You probably can find a template for this directive on a state web site, or the attorney completing the documents discussed above can provide you with a template. Don't forget to consider being an organ donor. I know it's a tough thing to think about, but consider who might benefit from a donated organ, it is one way for your life to continue being meaningful.

Beneficiary designations are often placed on products that we own and they tell the custodians of the product who should receive the asset at our demise. It's very important to review your beneficiary designations regularly, to avoid mistakes. For instance, if you're in a second marriage, and you die with your first spouse named as the beneficiary of your Life Insurance policy, it's possible that your grave site marker gets written as, "Here lies a no good husband," or something worse! Beyond assigning beneficiary designations to Life Insurance policies, I recommend doing so on investment accounts, and bank accounts. Be aware that sometimes institutions use the term Transfer on Death (TOD) rather than Beneficiary, but it pretty much accomplishes the same thing. By the way, Beneficiary Designations can help assets from going through the probate process so assets get distributed more quickly. Assigning or changing beneficiary designations can be done for no fee and is quick and easy!

Wealth Building Task

Wealth Building Task Ten: Create a list identifying the names and contact information of your key advisors: wealth coach/investment advisor, insurance agent, estate attorney, accountant, and banker. At some point it might be to your advantage to bring these key advisors together to make sure they are all working in a complementary fashion, toward your goal(s). My suggestion is to appoint your wealth coach as the captain, and allow them to coordinate with your other key advisors. As an example, if your wealth coach identifies the lack of estate planning documents e.g. Last Will and Testament, they can communicate with your attorney to have these documents completed.

Chapter 11

Ready, Set, Action

"An object at rest stays at rest."
Isaac Newton

Your Final Plan

If you have been diligent and completed all of the Wealth Building Tasks; you've already made enormous strides toward your destinations. At this point you have your working template, Next 30 Years Destinations and Road Map to Success to help guide you each day. But like going on a diet, it's easy to cheat. You skip one day and then another, and before you realize it, you're back to your old weight.

I want to give you a few "pearls" that have been passed down through the centuries, to help you stay focused on what's really important. Many consider the tools we're about to discuss as esoteric, only for a few selected people like kings. But that's nonsense, they are for anyone that trusts in their powers; powers that leaders, scholars, and world class athletes have used to achieve what others only dream of.

Commit

Remind yourself why you're following a Road Map to Success. How are you going to feel when you achieve each of your Next 30 Years Destinations? Commit to putting yourself in a position to win and succeed. We all face adversity at some time in our lives, but those that remain focused on their goal(s), and continually look to improve themselves, become the ultimate winner. Don't look for immediate results in your quest to build wealth. If it were that easy, there would be no need for this book and we'd all be incredibly wealthy!

Commit to your plan. I mean really, really, commit to following the steps outlined in your Road Map to Success, as though your life depends upon it. If you haven't placed a copy of your Next 30 Years Destinations and Road Map to Success where you'll review it daily, please do it now. Give a copy of each of these documents to someone you really trust, a spouse, family member, or friend, and explain to them just how very important your "Destinations" are to you. By doing this you will now be held accountable by these people, by virtue of the trust you have given them when you shared your destinations. They're not going to let you fail, only you can let yourself fail, and failure is not an option when you fully commit to your dreams.

Visualize

Visualization is a technique that has been used for centuries, and uses the brain to prepare the body to successfully complete meaningful activities. Some people describe visualization as merely day-dreaming, but Merriam-Webster Dictionary defines a "day-dream" as a pleasant visionary, usually wishful creation of the imagination. But being wishful requires no effort on your part, wishful people believe free lunches exist. No, your destinations are not wishful dreams, they have been developed using meaningful tools, such as SMAC, and they are supported by a Road Map to Success that does require effort.

Rather than simply reading and rereading your destinations and map each day, I'd like you to practice visualizing yourself following the steps in your Road Map, all the way to achieving your goal/destination. When you practice this technique, make it as vivid as you can. Create a clear mental picture of how you will feel as you complete tasks on the way to your destination. Picture your facial expression. Are you happy and smiling? Are loved ones around you celebrating your accomplishments? Notice the environment around you, trees, flowers etc. Engage as many senses in this vision as possible (sight, sound, smell, touch, and taste), and that all important feeling in your "gut". Don't worry if your picture isn't vivid initially, it will get better with practice.

At this point you might be skeptical of the benefits of visualization. You might be thinking that Spillane just "jumped the shark" with this stuff. However, you'd be surprised at the number of top athletes, actors, business people, and psychologists that recognize the powers of visualization, also known as Imagery Rehearsal. What do you think that baseball batter is doing when they step out of the batter's box? What is that golfer doing just before making that critical shot? Why is the cliff diver closing their eyes just before diving? How did an individual with a learning disability, and no college degree, build a personal net worth in the billions of dollars. They are visualizing their success and vividly seeing the steps necessary to achieve their goals. They can see, feel, taste, and sense the desired outcome. They're not thinking about failure, nor waiting for luck.

If you still think this is a crazy technique do a web search on this topic, you'll be surprised. Then, start practicing this technique every day; you may get a little "freaked out" when some of your outcomes occur exactly as you envisioned them. Make sure you focus on the whole experience, the steps leading up to success, including hard work, as well as the celebration itself. After all, why shouldn't you achieve your dreams? You have all the tools necessary, you just need to put them to use.

Once you begin to experience wealth building success, you'll set the bar a little higher, then, a little higher, eventually, achieving things you once thought impossible.

Wealth Building Task

Wealth Building Task Eleven: Put a copy of your "Next 30 Years Destinations" and "Roadmap to Success" in a place where you are going to review them daily e.g. computer screen, refrigerator, or on the bathroom mirror. Make it a daily activity to review these documents and practice the visualization techniques discussed in this chapter. Picture how you're going to feel as you achieve your destinations.

In addition, put an action on your calendar each month to review and update your expense budget statement.

Chapter 12

Achieving Self-Actualization

"Nothing can stop the man with a right mental attitude from achieving his goal.
Nothing on earth can help the man with the wrong mental attitude."
Thomas Jefferson

Evaluate

There is an old saying, "If at first you don't succeed, try, try, again." If you find yourself struggling to accomplish a goal, go back and ask why? Inspect what you expect! Does the goal fit the SMAC requirements? Do you need to alter your variables (G= R x T x I)? Do you need to change your Road Map, perhaps adding additional steps in order to succeed? Be critical, but don't be harsh on yourself. Ask the person or people that you have shared your Next 30 Years Destinations and Road Map to Success with, if they have any suggestions; you know they want to see you succeed!

Accentuate the Positive

Rome wasn't built in a day, and hindsight suggests it wasn't done without some errors. Embrace the lyrics written in 1944 and sung by Bing Crosby and the Andrews Sisters, "You got to accentuate the positive and eliminate the negative." Use the strategies we discussed earlier about redefining success:

- Going 3 for 10 as a batter makes you an All-star, and
- Getting 4 out of 5 questions correct on a math quiz gives you a B-.

Okay, you want to get A's, keep refining and working on goals.

Importantly, make sure you celebrate and accentuate your successes, no matter how big or small. Recognition of achievements is the fourth rung on Maslow's Hierarchy. Reward yourself when you achieve a goal, go to lunch at a favorite restaurant, buy yourself an ice cream, or maybe visit a loved one. If business, sports, and the entertainment industries recognize the value of celebrating accomplishments, via awards, shouldn't you?

Be Grateful!

Years ago someone taught me that if you're consciously grateful for the things in your life; you'll accomplish more. Having a negative attitude is mentally and physically draining, and a distraction from your destinations. I'll bet you have worked with someone that constantly complains about everything, right? I call that person Dan or Debbie "Downer". If you're around these people long enough, you can physically feel yourself getting sucked into their emotional state, and before you know it, you're complaining, too. By the end of the day, you're exhausted. It takes a lot of energy to be negative, doesn't it? Move away from these people, they're like a rat going down the drain and they're trying to take you with them. If you want to use your energy in a more productive way, start thinking about positive things in your life. Remind yourself of the things you are grateful for like your health, family, a pet, etc. When we have these good thoughts; our body releases chemicals that give us a natural "high" and it's free, and legal!

I suggest you create a "Grateful List", a list stating the things you are grateful for, and add to the list as you think of new ones. Each morning take a few minutes to review your grateful list, and use your new "visualization" skills to picture them. Believe me, you are going to find yourself smiling as you complete this task, and you're going to approach the day very differently than Dan and Debbie Downer. You'll experience more joy in life's tasks and your employer, peers, and loved ones will notice the difference. It won't take long before someone asks you why you're so happy, which will give you the opportunity to teach them the skills that have made you more productive and successful in life. Bye-bye Dan and Debbie Downer!

Law of Attraction and Abundance

The law of Attraction is a belief that you attract into your life what you think about, while the Law of Abundance states that there is an unlimited source of everything we need or want. Therefore, if we think deeply about the things we want in life, and understand that these things exist in ample supply; we can attract them. Too often we simply say, "I wish I could have "something. Stop wishing and start believing. You have the skills and power to attract whatever you commit to. If your goal is to build an investment portfolio worth millions of dollars, or you want to create a charitable foundation, start doing the things required. Complete a Next 30 Years Destinations sheet, and then add the required actions to your Road Map to Success sheet, practice referable traits, mime the wealthy (pick up the pennies), visualize your success, and be grateful.

Remember, there is plenty of whatever it is that you want, food, shelter, love, esteem, all leading you toward self-actualization.

Start with your destination in mind; follow the process, welcome the good things that come your way, and always remain humble!

Wealth Building Task

Wealth Building Task Twelve: Create a grateful list for yourself, at the bottom of the page write, "God don't make no junk," and "So, why not me?" Put your grateful list on your mirror and make it the first thing you review every day.

My Symphony
To live content with small means;
To seek elegance rather than luxury,
And refinement rather than fashion;
To be worthy, not respectable, and wealthy, not rich;
To study hard, think quietly,
Talk gently,
Act frankly;
To listen to stars and birds, to babes and sages, with open heart;
To bear all cheerfully,
Do all bravely,
Await occasions,
Hurry never.
In a word, to let the spiritual, unbidden and unconscious, grow up through the common.
This is to be my symphony.

William Henry Channing

Good luck, be nice, and be happy!

CPSIA information can be obtained at www.ICGtesting.com
Printed in the USA
BVOW02s1126311213

340560BV00006B/14/P